A Course for
Specialized English of Mechanics

力学专业英语

孟庆元　主编

哈尔滨工业大学出版社

内 容 简 介

本书从应力和应变的基本概念开始,介绍了有关静力学、动力学、弹性力学、塑性力学、材料力学行为和机理、计算和实验方法、断裂和疲劳、计算机以及民用和空间技术等诸多领域的专业知识,选材广泛,内容精练。

本书适合于工程力学及其他相关专业的大学本科生或研究生作专业英语教材,也可作为科技人员提高英语水平的阅读材料。

图书在版编目(CIP)数据

力学专业英语/孟庆元主编. —哈尔滨:哈尔滨工业大学出版社,2002.5(2023.1 重印)
ISBN 978-7-5603-1706-9

Ⅰ.力… Ⅱ.孟… Ⅲ.专业英语 Ⅳ.TB279

中国版本图书馆 CIP 数据核字(2002)第 26381 号

责任编辑	张晓京 杨明蕾
封面设计	卞秉利
出版发行	哈尔滨工业大学出版社
社　　址	哈尔滨市南岗区复华四道街 10 号　邮编 150006
传　　真	0451-86414749
网　　址	http://hitpress.hit.edu.cn
印　　刷	肇东市一兴印刷有限公司
开　　本	880mm×1230mm　1/32　印张 8.25　字数 198 千字
版　　次	2002 年 5 月第 1 版　2023 年 1 月第 11 次印刷
书　　号	ISBN 978-7-5603-1706-9
定　　价	28.00 元

(如因印装质量问题影响阅读,我社负责调换)

The Author

Qingyuan Meng, graduated in 1970 from Harbin Institute of Military Engineering, and in 1978 was matriculated as a postgraduate student of engineering mechanics in Harbin Institute of Technology. He went abroad to the University of Manchester, England, for postgraduate studies sponsored by the Chinese Government, in January 1980, and obtained the degree of Ph.D. in 1984. From 1991 to 1993, he carried out research on smart materials as a senior visiting scholar and research associate in the University of California at Santa Barbara, USA. He is now a professor, Ph.D. advisor of the subject of solid mechanics, in the Department of Astronautical Engineering and Mechanics, Harbin Institute of Technology. He is also the Chief Editor of the Journal of Harbin Institute of Technology (English Edition). He is currently teaching and working in the realm mainly related to the mechanics of solid materials, molecular design and molecular simulations, as well as numerical methods of computational mechanics.

作者简历

孟庆元，1970年毕业于哈尔滨军事工程学院，1978年考取哈尔滨工业大学工程力学专业研究生。1980年1月由国家公派赴英国曼彻斯特大学留学，并于1984年获得博士学位。1991～1993年在美国加州大学圣巴巴拉分校以高级访问学者和副研究员身份从事智能材料研究工作。现为哈尔滨工业大学航天工程与力学系教授，固体力学学科博士生指导教师，哈尔滨工业大学学报（英文版）主编。目前，在固体材料力学、分子设计与分子模拟以及计算力学方法等领域从事教学和研究工作。

Preface

This book is intended to be written and used to undergraduate students as a specialized English course in the realm of engineering mechanics and its related fields. The texts in this book are concerned with a wide range of subject matters relevant to various topics of mechanics. The typical technical terms, the grammatical structures and sentence patterns commonly used in scientific books and papers frequently occur throughout the book.

The special kind of English which is used only in science and technology has to be learned as a separate language. This is due to the fact that for students who learned English as a language of everyday conversation and of literature, it will be very difficult for them to understand what is written in specialized technical English. Therefore, the purpose of this course is to teach students of scientific subjects the basic language of technical English.

Technical English uses grammatical and syntactic forms and patterns which often occur in a formal style, with a very high concentration of technical terms and a number of mathematical symbols. In fact, many technical English words have been taken from everyday language but given a precise definition for technical use. In this case, the meanings of these words in their technical use are likely to differ from their non-technical meanings. As a result, technical English does differ from everyday English because of the specialized contexts. However, as far as technical English is concerned, the differences will not present any great problems once the features of technical English have been learned and recognized.

The learning approach of the book is recommended to be essentially an oral practice, in view of the fact that oral repetition is the most effective way of fixing material, even for purely recognition purpose. In addition to the purely language-teaching aims outlined above, the book is also recommended to be used to stimulate critical thought and foster the habits of clear exposition of ideas and the impartial assessment of evidence.

Finally, it is hopeful that the texts in this book are shown in such a way that will be of interest to the students who pursue the subject of mechanics for learning both the language of specialized technical English and the knowledge of mechanics.

Q. Meng

序　言

　　本书是为工程力学及其他相关专业大学本科生专业英语教学而编写的教材。书中的课文涉及到了力学学科中的许多领域。有关的专业术语以及在科学文献中常见的科技英语句型和语法结构都贯穿于本书中。

　　由于专业科技英语属于科技领域中的专门的语言范畴，具有一定的特殊性，因此，在学习中应把专业英语看做是与一般日常英语不同的另一种形式的语言。事实上，对于学习日常英语和文学的学生来说，他们很难理解专业科技英语的涵义。因此，编写本书的目的就是对科技专业的大学生们进行专业英语知识的基本训练。

　　专业科技英语的语法和句式往往十分规范和严谨。在科学文献中充满了大量的科技专业术语和数学符号。事实上，许多科技英语词汇来源于日常英语，但在科技文献中却具有十分严格且独立的定义。在这种情况下，这些作为科技专业英语使用的词汇的涵义与作为日常生活用语时的意义截然不同，这完全取决于语言的环境。然而，通过学习只要对科技专业英语的特征有所认识，这种差异将不会成为学习专业英语的困难。

　　关于本书的学习方法，作者建议以口语训练为主。这是由于不断重复的口语训练可以深入地认知和理解事物。除以上所说的纯粹语言训练外，作者还建议通过本教材的学习，激发学生思维的积极性，培养学生准确表述思想和公正评价某个事物的能力。

　　最后，希望学习工程力学及其他相关专业的大学生们通过本教材的训练，不仅在科技专业英语学习方面，也同时在有关力学专业知识的学习方面产生浓厚的兴趣。

编　者
2002 年 5 月 30 日

Contents

Lesson 1	Stress and Strain	(1)
Lesson 2	Tensile Stress-strain Behavior	(6)
Lesson 3	Torsion of A Circular Bar	(10)
Lesson 4	Deflections of Beams	(14)
Lesson 5	Gravitation in the Universe	(19)
Lesson 6	Equilibrium of Rigid Bodies	(24)
Lesson 7	Newton's Laws of Motion	(29)
Lesson 8	The Planar Motion of A Rigid Body	(33)
Lesson 9	Theorems of Particle Dynamics	(39)
Lesson 10	Vibrations of A Single Particle	(44)
Lesson 11	Stress Equilibrium and Compatibility	(49)
Lesson 12	Elastic Constitutive Relations	(54)
Lesson 13	Stress Concentrations	(60)
Lesson 14	Buckling of Columns	(66)
Lesson 15	What Are Dynamic Problems?	(71)
Lesson 16	General Description of Waves	(75)
Lesson 17	Potential Energy Method	(80)
Lesson 18	Principle of Virtual Work	(85)
Lesson 19	Introduction to Computer Hardware	(90)
Lesson 20	Introduction to Computer Software	(95)
Lesson 21	Metallic Materials	(99)
Lesson 22	Nonmetallic Materials	(104)
Lesson 23	Composite Materials	(110)
Lesson 24	Behavior of Composite Materials	(115)

Lesson 25	Basic Deformations of Materials	(120)
Lesson 26	Failure Modes of Materials	(124)
Lesson 27	Plastic Behavior of A Tensile Bar	(128)
Lesson 28	Yield Criteria	(134)
Lesson 29	Plastic Flow Rule	(139)
Lesson 30	Plastic Limit Analysis	(145)
Lesson 31	Mechanisms of Elastic Deformation	(150)
Lesson 32	Mechanisms of Plastic Deformation	(155)
Lesson 33	Finite Element Method	(160)
Lesson 34	Programming A Problem Solution	(165)
Lesson 35	Experimental Techniques	(171)
Lesson 36	Photoelasticity	(177)
Lesson 37	Fracture of Brittle Materials	(182)
Lesson 38	Linear Elastic Fracture Mechanics	(187)
Lesson 39	Ductile Fracture	(192)
Lesson 40	Fatigue in Metals	(196)
Lesson 41	Time-Dependent Deformation in Solids	(202)
Lesson 42	Viscous Behavior of Polymers	(207)
Lesson 43	Creep in Metals	(212)
Lesson 44	Friction and Wear of Materials	(217)
Lesson 45	Basic Equations of Fluid Mechanics	(222)
Lesson 46	Civil Engineering	(227)
Lesson 47	The Airplanes	(232)
Lesson 48	Communications Satellites	(237)
Lesson 49	Travel into Outer Space	(241)
Lesson 50	Courses of Mechanics in UMIST	(245)

参考文献 (252)

Lesson 1

Stress and Strain

1. The concepts of stress and strain can be illustrated in an elementary way by considering the extension of a prismatic bar. As shown in Fig.1, a prismatic bar is one that has constant cross section throughout its length and a straight axis. In this illustration the bar is assumed to be loaded at its ends by axial forces P that produce a uniform stretching, or tension, of the bar.

2. By making an artificial cut (section mm) through the bar at right angles to its axis, we can isolate part of the bar as a free body [see Fig.1(b)]. At the left-hand end the tensile force P is applied, and at the other end there are forces representing

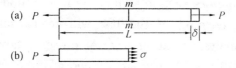

Fig.1 Prismatic bar in tension

the action of the removed portion of the bar upon the part that remains. These forces will be continuously distributed over the cross section, analogous to the continuous distribution of hydrostatic pressure over a submerged surface.

· 1 ·

3. The intensity of force, that is, the force per unit area, is called the stress and is commonly denoted by the Greek letter σ. Assuming that the stress has a uniform distribution over the cross section [see Fig.1(b)], we can readily see that its resultant is equal to the intensity σ times the cross-sectional area A of the bar. Furthermore, from the equilibrium of the body shown in Fig.1(b), we can also see that this resultant must be equal in magnitude and opposite in direction to the force P. Hence, we obtain

$$\sigma = \frac{P}{A} \qquad (1)$$

4. Eq. (1) can be regarded as the equation for the uniform stress in a prismatic bar. This equation shows that stress has units of force divided by area. When the bar is being stretched by the force P, as shown in the figure, the resulting stress is a tensile stress; if the forces are reversed in direction, causing the bar to be compressed, they are called compressive stresses.

5. A necessary condition for Eq. (1) to be valid is that the stress σ must be uniform over the cross section of the bar. This condition will be realized if the axial force P acts through the centroid of the cross section. When the load P does not act at the centroid, bending of the bar will result, and a more complicated analysis is necessary. At present, however, it is assumed that all axial forces are applied at the centroid of the cross section unless specifically stated to the contrary. Also, unless stated otherwise, it is generally assumed that the weight of the object itself is neglected, as was done when discussing the bar in Fig.1.

6. The total elongation of a bar carrying an axial force will

be denoted by the Greek letter δ [see Fig.1(a)], and the elongation per unit length, or strain, is then determined by the equation

$$\varepsilon = \frac{\delta}{L} \qquad (2)$$

where L is the total length of the bar. Note that the strain ε is a non-dimensional quantity. It can be obtained accurately from Eq. (2) as long as the strain is uniform throughout the length of the bar. If the bar is in tension, the strain is a tensile strain, representing an elongation or stretching of the material; if the bar is in compression, the strain is a compressive strain, which means that adjacent cross sections of the bar move closer to one another.

7. When a material exhibits a linear relationship between stress and strain, it is said to be linear elastic. This is an extremely important property of many solid materials, including most metals, plastics, wood, concrete, and ceramics. The linear relationship between stress and strain for a bar in tension can be expressed by the simple equation

$$\sigma = E\varepsilon \qquad (3)$$

in which E is a constant of proportionality known as the modulus of elasticity for the material.

8. Note that E has the same units as stress. The modulus of elasticity is sometimes called Young's modulus, after the English scientist Thomas Young (1773 ~ 1829) who studied the elastic behavior of bars. For most materials the modulus of elasticity in compression is the same as in tension.

New Words and Expressions

analogous [ə'næləgəs] *adj.* 类似的，相似的
artificial [ˌɑːti'fiʃəl] *adj.* 人工的，人造的，假的
centroid ['sentrɔid] *n.* 质心，形心
ceramic [si'ræmik] *adj.* 陶瓷的；*n.* 陶瓷(制品)
compress [kəm'pres] *v.* 压缩，压紧
compressive [kəm'presiv] *adj.* 压缩的，有压缩力的
concrete ['kɔnkriːt] *n.* 混凝土
contrary ['kɔntrəri] *adj.* 相反的，逆的；*n.* 反面；*adv.* 相反地
distribute [dis'tribjuːt] *vt.* 分布，散布
elasticity [elæs'tisiti] *n.* 弹力，弹性
elongation [ˌiːlɔŋ'geiʃən] *n.* 伸长，延伸
equation [i'kweiʃən] *n.* 方程，等式
equilibrium [ˌiːkwi'libriəm] *n.* 平衡
hydrostatics [ˌhaidrəu'stætiks] *n.* 流体静力学
intensity [in'tensiti] *n.* 强度，强烈
isolate ['aisəleit] *vt.* 使隔离，使绝缘
linear ['liniə] *adj.* 线性的，直线的
modulus ['mɔdjuləs] *n.* 模量，模数
pressure ['preʃə] *n.* 压，压力，压迫，强制，紧迫
prismatic [priz'mætik] *adj.* 棱镜的，棱柱形的
proportionality [prəˌpɔːʃə'næliti] *n.* 比例
resultant [ri'zʌltənt] *adj.* 合成的；*n.* 合力
solid ['sɔlid] *n.* 固体；*adj.* 固体的，坚固的，稳固的
strain [strein] *n.* 应变

stress [stres] *n*. 应力

stretch [stretʃ] *vt*. 伸展，伸张，展开，把……拉直(长)

submerge [səb'mə:dʒ] *v*. 浸没，淹没；*vi*. 潜水

tension ['tenʃən] *n*. 张力，拉力，拉紧

Lesson 2

Tensile Stress-strain Behavior

1. The relationship between stress and strain in a particular material is determined by means of a tensile test. A specimen of the material, usually in the form of a round bar, is placed in a testing machine and subjected to tension. The force on the bar and the elongation of the bar are measured as the load is increased. The stress in the bar is found by dividing the force by the cross-sectional area, and the strain is found by dividing the elongation by the length along which the elongation occurs. In this manner a complete stress-strain diagram can be obtained for the material.

2. The typical shape of the stress-strain diagram for structural steel is shown in Fig.1, where the axial strains are

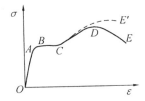

Fig.1 A typical stress-strain curve

plotted on the horizontal axis and the corresponding stresses are given by the ordinates to the curve $OABCDE$. From O to A the stress and strain are directly proportional to one another and the diagram is linear. Beyond point A the linear relationship between stress and strain no longer exists, hence the stress at A is called the proportional limit.

3. With an increase in loading, the strain increases more rapidly than the stress, until at point B a considerable elongation begins to occur with no appreciable increase in the tensile force. This phenomenon is known as yielding of the material, and the stress at point B is called the yield point or yield stress. In the region BC the material is said to have become plastic, and the bar may actually elongate plastically by an amount which is 10 or 15 times the elongation which occurs up to the proportional limit.

4. At point C the material begins to strain harden and to offer additional resistance to increase in load. Thus, with further elongation the stress increases, and it reaches its maximum value, or ultimate stress, at point D. Beyond this point further stretching of the bar is accompanied by a reduction in the load, and fracture of the specimen finally occurs at point E on the diagram.

5. During elongation of the bar a lateral contraction occurs, resulting in a decrease in the cross-sectional area of the

Fig.2 Necking of a bar in tension

bar. This phenomenon has no effect on the stress-strain diagram up to about point C, but beyond that point the decease in area will have a noticeable effect upon the calculated value of stress. A pronounced necking of the bar occurs (see Fig.2), and if the actual cross-sectional area at the narrow part of the neck is used in calculating σ, it will be found that the true stress-strain curve follows the dashed line CE. Whereas the total load the bar can carry does indeed diminish after the ultimate stress is reached (line DE), this reduction is due to the decrease in area and not to a loss in strength of the material itself.

6. The material actually withstands an increase in stress up to the point of failure. For most practical purposes, however, the conventional stress-strain curve $OABCDE$, based upon the original cross-sectional area of the specimen, provides satisfactory information for design purposes.

7. The diagram in Fig.1 has been drawn to show the general characteristics of the stress-strain curve. There is an initial region on the stress-strain curve in which the material behaves both elastically and linearly. The region from O to A on the stress-strain diagram for steel is an example. The presence of a pronounced yield point followed by large plastic strains is somewhat unique to steel, which is the most common structural metal in use today. Aluminium alloys exhibit a more gradual transition from the linear to the nonlinear region.

8. Both steel and many aluminium alloys will undergo large strains before failure and are therefore classified as ductile. On the other hand, materials that are brittle fail at relatively low values of strain. Examples include ceramics, cast iron, concrete, certain metallic alloys, and glass.

New Words and Expressions

alloy ['ælɔi] n. 合金
aluminium [ˌælju:'minjəm] n. 铝
appreciable [ə'pri:ʃiəbl] adj. 可感知的, 可评估的
axial ['æksiəl,-sjəl] adj. 轴的, 轴向的
brittle ['britl] adj. 脆性的, 易碎的
characteristic [ˌkæriktə'ristik] adj. 特有的, 典型的; n. 特性, 特征
contraction [kən'trækʃən] n. 收缩, 减缩
diminish [di'miniʃ] v. (使)减少, (使)变小
ductile ['dʌktail] adj. 易延展的, 韧性的
effect [i'fekt] n. 效果; vt. 影响
failure ['feiljə] n. 失败, 破坏, 失效
harden ['ha:dn] vt. 使变硬, 使坚强; vi. 变硬, 变冷酷
horizontal [ˌhɔri'zɔntl] adj. 水平的, 水平线的
lateral ['lætərəl] adj. 侧面的, 横向的
limit ['limit] n. 界限; vt. 限定
neck [nek] n. 脖子, 颈, 颈壮物; vi. 收缩, 颈缩
necking ['nekiŋ] n. 颈缩
phenomenon [fi'nɔminən] n. 现象
plastic ['plæstik, pla:stik] adj. 塑性的
plot [plɔt] n. 地图, 图; vt. 划, 绘图, 密谋; vi. 密谋, 策划
reduction [ri'dʌkʃən] n. 减少
resistance [ri'zistəns] n. 抵抗力, 阻力, 电阻, 反抗
specimen ['spesimin,-mən] n. 试件
transition [træn'ziʒən,-'siʃən] n. 转变, 转换
ultimate ['ʌltimit] adj. 极限的, 终极的
withstand [wið'stænd] vt. 抵住, 经得起
yield [ji:ld] n. 屈服; v. 产出, 生产; vi. (~ to) 屈服于, 屈从

Lesson 3

Torsion of A Circular Bar

1. Let us consider a bar of circular cross section twisted by couples T acting at the ends (see Fig.1). A bar loaded in this manner is said to be in pure torsion. It can be shown from considerations of symmetry that cross sections of the circular bar rotate as rigid bodies about the longitudinal axis, with radii remaining straight and the cross sections remaining circular. Also, if the total angle of twist of the bar is small, neither the length of the bar nor its radius r will change.

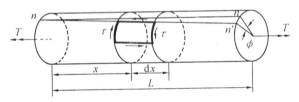

Fig.1 Circular bar in pure torsion

2. During torsion there will be a rotation about the longitudinal axis of one end of the bar with respect to the other. For instance, if we consider the left-hand end of the bar as fixed, then the right-hand end will rotate through an angle ϕ with respect to the left end. At the same time, a longitudinal line on the surface of the bar, such as line nn, will rotate

through a small angle to the position nn'. Because of this rotation, a rectangular element on the surface of the bar, such as the element shown in the figure between two cross sections distance $\mathrm{d}x$ apart, is distorted into a rhomboid.

3. When a shaft is subjected to pure torsion, the rate of change $\mathrm{d}\phi/\mathrm{d}x$ of the angle of twist is constant along the length of the bar. This constant represents the angle of twist per unit length and will be denoted by θ. Thus, we see that $\theta = \phi/L$, where L is the length of the shaft. Then, the shear strain γ is obtained by

$$\gamma = r\theta = r\phi/L \qquad (1)$$

The shear stresses τ which act on the sides of the element have the directions shown in Fig.1. For a linear elastic material, the magnitude of the shear stress is

$$\tau = G\gamma = Gr\theta \qquad (2)$$

Equations (1) and (2) relate the strain and stress at the surface of the shaft to the angle of twist per unit length.

4. The state of stress within the interior of the shaft can be determined in a manner similar to that used for the surface of the shaft. Because radii in the cross sections of the bar remain straight and undistorted during twisting, we see that an interior element situated on the surface of an interior cylinder of radius ρ is also in pure shear with the corresponding shear strain and stress being given by the following expressions

$$\gamma = \rho\theta \qquad \tau = G\rho\theta \qquad (3\mathrm{a,b})$$

These equations show that the shear strain and shear stress vary linearly with the radial distance ρ from the center of the shaft and have their maximum values at the outer surface.

5. The shear stresses acting in the plane of the cross

section, given by Eq. (3b), are accompanied by equal shear stresses acting on longitudinal planes of the shaft. This result follows from the fact that equal shear stresses always exist on mutually perpendicular planes. If a material is weaker in shear longitudinally than laterally (for example, wood), the first cracks in a twisted shaft will appear on the surface in the longitudinal direction.

6. The state of pure shear stress on the surface of the shaft is equivalent to equal tensile and compressive stresses on an element rotated through an angle of 45° to the axis of the shaft. If a material that is weaker in tension than in shear is twisted, failure occurs in tension along a helix inclined at 45° the axis. This type of failure can easily be demonstrated by twisting a piece of chalk.

7. The relationship between the applied torque T and the angle of twist which it produces will now be established. The resultant of the shear stresses must be statically equivalent to the total torque T. The shear force acting on an element of area dA is τdA, and the moment of this force about the axis of the bar is $\tau_\rho dA$. Using Eq. (3b), this moment is also equal to $G\theta\rho^2 dA$. The total torque T is the summation over the entire cross-sectional area of such elemental moments, thus

$$T = \int G\theta\rho^2 dA = G\theta \int \rho^2 dA = G\theta J \qquad (4)$$

where $J = \int \rho^2 dA$ is the polar moment of inertia of the circular cross section. From Eq. (4) we obtain $\theta = T/GJ$ which shows that θ, the angle of twist per unit length, varies directly with the torque T and inversely with the product GJ, known as the torsional rigidity of the shaft.

New Words and Expressions

couple ['kʌpl] n. 对, 力偶; v. 耦连, 耦合
crack [kræk] n. 裂缝, 裂纹; v. (使)破裂, (使)爆裂
cylinder ['silində] n. 圆筒, 圆筒状物
distort [dis'tɔːt] vt. 扭曲, 歪曲使变形, 弄歪, 曲解, 使失真
helix ['hiːliks] n. 螺旋, 螺旋状物
inertia [i'nəːʃjə] n. 惯性, 惯量, 惰性
longitudinal [lɔndʒi'tjuːdinl] adj. 纵向的, 经线的
moment ['məumənt] n. 力矩, 瞬间; adj. 片刻的, 瞬间的, 力矩的
perpendicular [ˌpəːpən'dikjulə] adj. 垂直的, 正交的; n. 垂线
polar ['pəulə] adj. 极性的, 两极的
radius ['reidjəs] n. 半径
rhomboid ['rɔmbɔid] n. 长菱形
rigidity [ri'dʒiditi] n. 刚性, 刚度, 坚硬, 僵硬, 严格, 严厉
rotate [rəu'teit] vi. 旋转, 循环, 轮换; vt. 使旋转[轮转]; 使循环, 使轮流
shaft [ʃaːft] n. 轴, 杆状物
torque [tɔːk] n. 扭矩, 扭力矩; 转矩, 转力矩
torsion ['tɔːʃən] n. 扭矩
twist [twist] vt. 扭, 拧, 使扭转; n. 扭曲

Lesson 4

Deflections of Beams

1. A bar that is subjected to forces acting transverse to its axis is called a beam. The beam in Fig. 1, with a pin support at one end and a roller support at the other, is called a simply supported beam, or a simple beam. The essential feature of a simple beam is that both ends of the beam may rotate freely during bending, but they cannot translate in the lateral direction. Also, one end of the beam can move freely in the axial direction. The beam, which is built-in or fixed at one end and free at the other end, is called a cantilever beam. At the fixed support the beam can neither rotate nor translate, while at the free end it may do both.

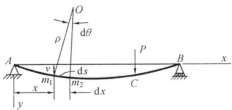

Fig.1 Deflection curve of a bent beam

2. Loads on a beam may be classified into concentrated force, such as P in Fig.1, or distributed loads which is expressed in units of force per unit distance along the axis of

the beam. The axial force N acting normal to the cross section and passing through the centroid of the cross section, shear force V acting parallel to the cross section, and bending moment M acting in the plane of the beam are known as stress resultants.

3. The relationship between the shear force V, bending moment M, and the loads on a beam is given by

$$\frac{\mathrm{d}M}{\mathrm{d}x} = V \tag{1}$$

This equation shows that the rate of change of the bending moment is equal to the algebraic value of the shear force, provided that a distributed load (or no load) acts on the beam. If the beam is acted upon by a concentrated force, however, there will be an abrupt change, or discontinuity, in the shear force at the point of application of the concentrated force.

4. Lateral loads acting on a beam will cause the beam to deflect. As shown in Fig.1, before the load P is applied, the longitudinal axis of the beam is straight. After bending, the axis of the beam becomes a curve, as represented by the line ACB. Let us assume that the xy plane is a plane of symmetry of the beam and that all loads act in this plane. Then the curve ACB, called the deflection curve of the beam, will lie in this plane also.

5. From the geometry of the figure we see that

$$K = \frac{1}{\rho} = \frac{\mathrm{d}\theta}{\mathrm{d}s} \tag{2}$$

where K is the curvature, equal to the reciprocal of the radius of curvature ρ. Thus, the curvature K is equal to the rate of change of the angle θ with respect to the distance s measured along the deflection curve.

6. The basic differential equation for the deflection curve of a beam is given as follows:

$$\frac{d^2v}{dx^2} = -\frac{M}{EI} \tag{3}$$

where v is the deflection of the beam from its initial position. It must be integrated in each particular case to find the deflection v. The procedure consists of successive integration of the equations, with the resulting constants of integration being evaluated from the boundary conditions of the beam. It should be realized that Eq.(3) is valid only when Hooke's law applies for the material and when the slopes of the deflection curve are very small.

7. Another method for finding deflections of beams is the moment-area method. The name of this method comes from the fact that it utilizes the area of the bending moment diagram. This method is especially suitable when it is desired to find the deflection or slope at only one point of the beam rather than finding the complete equation of the deflection curve.

8. The normal and shear stresses acting at any point in the cross section of a beam can be obtained by using the equations

$$\sigma_x = \frac{My}{I}, \tau = \frac{VQ}{Ib} \tag{4a,b}$$

in which I is the second moment (or the moment of inertia) of the cross-sectional area with respect to the neutral axis, and Q is the first moment (or static moment) of the plane area of a beam. It can be seen that the normal stress is a maximum at the outer edges of the beam and is zero at the neutral axis; the shear stress is zero at the outer edges and usually reaches a maximum at the neutral axis.

9. The shear force V and bending moment M in a beam will usually vary with the distance x defining the location of the cross section at which they occur. When designing a beam, it is desirable to know the values of V and M at all cross sections of the beam, and a convenient way to provide this information is by a graph showing how they vary along the axis of the beam. To plot the graph, we take the abscissa as the position of the cross section, and we take the ordinate as the corresponding value of either the shear force or the bending moment. Such graphs are called shear force and bending moment diagrams.

10. The simple beam shown in Fig. 1 is one of the statically determinate beams. The feature of this type of beams is that all their reactions can be determined from equations of static equilibrium. The beams that have a large number of reactions than the number of equations of static equilibrium are said to be statically indeterminate. For statically determinate beams we could immediately obtain the reactions of the beam by solving equations of static equilibrium. However, when the beam is statically indeterminate, we cannot solve for the forces on the basis of statics alone. Instead, we must take into account the deflections of the beam and obtain equations of compatibility to supplement the equations of statics.

New Words and Expressions

abrupt [ə'brʌpt] *adj.* 突然的,突变的,不连续的
abscissa [æb'sisə] *n.* 横坐标
boundary ['baundəri] *n.* 边界,分界线
cantilever ['kæntiliːvə] *n.* 悬臂(梁),伸臂

compatibility [kəmˌpæti'biliti] n. 相容性,协调性
concentrate ['kɔnsentreit] v. 集中,浓缩,凝缩;专心
curvature ['kə:vətʃə] n. 曲率,弯曲
deflection [di'flekʃən] n. 挠度,挠曲;偏转,偏斜
determinate [di'tə:minit] adj. 确定的,决定的;n. 行列式
differential [ˌdifə'renʃəl] adj. 微分的,差别的;n. 微分
discontinuity ['disˌkɔnti'nju(:)iti] n. 间断,不连续
distribute [dis'tribju(:)t] vt. 分布,散布,分配
equilibrium [ˌi:kwi'libriəm] n. 平衡,均衡
indeterminate [ˌindi'tə:minit] adj. 不确定的
initial [i'niʃəl] adj. 开始的;最初的
integrate ['intigreit] vt. 使成整体,使一体化,求⋯的积分;
　　　　　v. 结合,综合,集成
lateral ['lætərəl] n. 侧部,支线;adj. 横(向)的,侧面的
longitudinal [lɔndʒi'tju:dinl] adj. 纵向的,经线的
neutral ['nju:trəl] adj. 中性的
normal ['nɔ:məl] adj. 正常的,正规的,法向的
ordinate ['ɔ:dinit] n. 纵坐标
radius ['reidjəs] n. 半径
reciprocal [ri'siprəkəl] adj. 倒数的,彼此相反的
resultant [ri'zʌltənt] adj. 合成的,结果的;n. 合力,生成物
rotate [rəu'teit] v. (使)旋转,(使)循环,(使)轮回
slope [sləup] n. 斜率,倾斜
statics ['stætiks] n. 静力学;静止状态,静态
successive [sək'sesiv] adj. 连续的,接连的,相继的
symmetry ['simitri] n. 对称
translate [træns'leit] v. 翻译,解释;转化,变换;转移,中继;
　　　　　移动,平移
transverse ['trænzvə:s] adj. 横向的,横断的

Lesson 5

Gravitation in the Universe

1. We are so used to our life on the surface of the earth that it can be quite an effort for our minds to break free of all the ideas that we take for granted. We talk about 'up' and 'down', but we know that what is 'down' for us is 'up' for someone else on the other side of the world. We can feel that things are heavy, and we often think of 'weight' as being a fixed quality in an object, but it is not really fixed at all. If you could take a one-pound packet of butter 4,000 miles out from the earth, it would weigh only a quarter of a pound.

2. Why would things weigh only a quarter as much as they do at the surface of the earth if we took them 4,000 miles out into space? The reason is this: All objects have a natural attraction for all other objects, this is called gravitational attraction. But the power of attraction between two objects gets weaker as they get farther apart.

3. What about the weight of our one-pound packet of butter on the surface of the moon? On the moon there will be an attraction between the butter and the moon, but the butter will weigh only about one-sixth as much as it does on the earth. This is because the moon is so much smaller than the earth. The amount of gravitational pull that a body produces depends on

the amount of material in it. So this is one of the first things we need to remember: that the weight of an object in space is not the same as its weight on the surface of the earth.

4. Gravitation is a very important force in the universe. Every object has a gravitational pull, which is rather like magnetism. But, unlike magnetism, gravitation is not found only in iron and steel, it is in every object large or small. But large objects, such as the earth, have a stronger pull than small ones. Sir Isaac Newton, the great scientist of the seventeenth century, first studied gravitation. When he was a boy, he often saw apples falling to the ground. He wondered why they fell towards the earth, and why they did not fly up into the sky.

5. According to the law which he later produced, everything in the universe attracts everything else towards itself. The sun attracts the earth and the earth attracts the sun. The earth attracts the moon and the moon attracts the earth. Although the bigger object has the stronger attraction, all objects in fact have some. But we do not notice the gravitational pull of a piece of butter because the pull of the earth is very much greater.

6. Why does the earth always move round the sun, and not fly off into cold space? The sun's gravitation gives the answer. The earth is always trying to move away in a straight line, but the sun is always pulling it back. So it continues on its journey round and round the sun.

7. The earth is in a great group of stars. We call this group the galaxy. The sun is one of the stars in the galaxy, in which there are about 100,000 million stars. It is not in the middle of the galaxy, but rather near one edge. These stars form a group,

the shape of which is rather like the shape of a watch. Outside the galaxy there is empty space, but thousands of millions of miles away there is another galaxy. Light from this other galaxy reaches us after about 2 million years.

8.In fact, there are millions of these galaxies in the universe, and they appear to be rushing away from us. Many astronomers believe that there are thousands of millions of millions of suns and some of these suns have planets as our sun does. The astronomers at Mount Palomar and Mount Wilson can see some of them well, but they cannot see one as it is now. The light takes millions of years to arrive here, so they see a distant galaxy as it used to be. The light left it millions of years ago. It traveled across space and then went into an astronomer's eye. Perhaps no men were living when it started.

9.Gravitation is the force which holds all the atoms of a star together. It holds the sun together and it holds the atoms of the earth together. It holds us on the earth. If there were no gravitation, we and everything else would fly off the earth into space.

10.Einstein produced a new law of gravitation. Its main results are the same as the results of Newton's law. But in very small and fine matters, Einstein's law gives different results. One of these is that gravitation bends light a little. But according to Newton's law gravitation has very little effect on light. Einstein showed this fact by means of mathematics, and not by experiment.

11.This result of his law was tested during an eclipse of the sun. Usually, when the light of a star passes the sun, we cannot see it, the sun is too bright. But sometimes the earth moves between the sun and the moon. Then the earth's shadow falls on the moon, no light from the sun can then reach the moon. The moon gets dark because it cannot reflect the sun's light. We call this an eclipse of the moon.

12. Sometimes the moon goes in front of the sun. We can watch its edge when it slowly crossed the sun's disc. Everything gets darker and darker. Then, at last, we cannot see any part of the sun's disc. The moon is hiding it completely. That is a total eclipse of the sun. Sometimes only part of the sun's disc is hidden, that is not a total eclipse. It is a partial eclipse of the sun. During an eclipse of the sun, the sun's light is shut out by the moon, then we can see the light of the star.

13. A ray of light usually travels in a straight line, but sometimes it bends. As shown in Fig.1, the astronomers who watched noticed that the star appeared to change its position a little. The cause of this was that the star's light was turning from the straight line as it passed the sun. The sun's gravitation was bending the beam of light. This showed that Einstein was right.

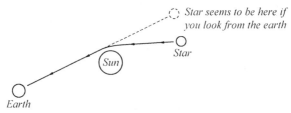

Fig.1 The light of a star passing the sun

New Words and Expressions

astronomer [əs'trɔnəmə(r)] n. 天文学家
atom ['ætəm] n. 原子
attraction [ə'trækʃən] n. 吸引,吸引力,引力
beam [biːm] n. 横梁,杆,光线
bend [bend] v. 弯曲,使弯曲; n. 弯曲,弯曲物,转弯
disc [disk] n. 圆盘,唱片
eclipse [i'klips] n. 日食,月食; v. 遮挡,重叠
edge [edʒ] n. 边缘,边, 棱, 边界, 界线, 刀刃
galaxy ['gæləksi] n. 天河, 银河, 星系
grant [graːnt] vt. 同意, 准予, 承认(…为真), 假定(…正确); n. 同意,准许,赠款,补助金
gravitation [ˌgrævi'teiʃən] n. 重力, 引力, 地心吸力
magnetism ['mægnitizəm] n. 磁性,磁学
object ['ɔbdʒikt] n. 物体,目标,对象
 [əb'dʒekt] vi. 反对,拒绝; vt. 提出 … 来反对
partial ['paːʃəl] adj. 部分的,偏(导数)的
planet ['plænit] n. 行星
pound [paund] n. 磅; 英镑
quality ['kwɔliti] n. 品质,质量,特性
ray [rei] n. 光线, 射线
reflect [ri'flekt] vt. 反射,反映; 招致, 带来
shadow ['ʃædəu] n. 阴影, 影子; vt. 遮蔽
shut [ʃʌt] v. 关闭, 关上; n. 关闭, 闭锁, 终止
universe ['juːnivəːs] n. 宇宙, 世界, 万物, 领域

Lesson 6

Equilibrium of Rigid Bodies

1. A primary goal in Statics is to establish the basic laws governing the forces acting on bodies that are in a state of equilibrium. One aid in describing forces required to prevent a body from moving is the free body diagram which isolates the body of interest from its surroundings. In the diagram we show all forces being exerted on the body, bearing in mind that Newton's third law tells us that forces are the result of the interaction between bodies. The process of constructing the diagram aids us in understanding which parameters of the system are important.

2. It is part of the task of constructing a free body diagram to examine the supports in order to deduce what types of force they apply to the body. These forces are sometimes called constraint forces, because they represent the way that the supports constrain the body from moving. Another term for these forces is reactions, because they represent the way in which the supports react to the tendency of the body to move. The restriction against movement is imposed by a reaction force, and the restriction against rotation is imposed by a reaction couple. Whenever the type of support allows the body to move in a specific direction, or rotate about a specific axis,

there will be no reaction force, or couple, in that direction.

3. We could develop a mathematical derivation of the criteria that must be satisfied if a body is to be in a state of static equilibrium. Before we investigate the relationship between the forces acting on a body in static equilibrium, let us visualize replacing the actual forces acting on a body by an equivalent force-couple system acting at some convenient point C. The force R, which is the sum of the actual forces, describes the resultant pushing or pulling effect on point C. The couple is the sum of the moments about point C of the actual forces. This couple describes the resultant tendency of the actual forces to cause the body to rotate about point C. The concept of static equilibrium of a rigid body is that there is no tendency for the body to move. In order for a rigid body to be in a state of static equilibrium it follows that the system of forces acting on the body must have both a zero resultant force and a zero resultant couple.

4. The most direct way of setting the resultant force and couple equal to zero is to actually compute the sum of the forces and the sum of the moments about any arbitrary point. We then equate the two resultant vectors to zero, thus obtaining

$$\sum F = 0, \qquad \sum M_c = 0 \qquad (1)$$

In the case of a three-dimensional force system, the force and moment sums have three components each, so Eqs. (1) are equivalent to the following six scalar equations of static equilibrium.

$$\sum F_x = 0, \qquad \sum F_y = 0, \qquad \sum F_z = 0 \qquad (2a)$$

$$\sum F_{cx} = 0, \qquad \sum F_{cy} = 0, \qquad \sum F_{cz} = 0 \qquad (2b)$$

The equilibrium equations for the case of a concurrent system of forces are a special case of eqs. $(2a, b)$ as may be seen by letting point C be the point of concurrency.

5. A solution to the equations of static equilibrium yields the reactions and other unknown forces appearing in a free body diagram. The choice of the point C for summing moments is arbitrary. We shall generally choose point C to be along the line of action of at least one unknown reaction, in order to eliminate that unknown from the moment equation. This procedure simplifies the equations to be solved. This ability to simplify the equations suggests that we consider alternative formulations in which moments are summed about more than one point.

6. In the case of a planar force system, there are only three nontrivial scalar equations of static equilibrium. These equations may be obtained from either of three alternative formulations, as follows:

(a) Equate to zero the moment about one point and the force sums in two directions. This is the approach of Eqs.(2a,b).

(b) Equate to zero the moment sums about two points and the force sum in a direction that is not perpendicular to the line connecting the two chosen points.

(c) Equate to zero the moment sums about three points that are not collinear.

For the case of a three-dimensional system of forces, the simplification would not be necessary, since the determination of moments in the three-dimensional case is somewhat lengthier than that for planar forces.

New Words and Expressions

alternative [ɔːlʹtəːnətiv] n. 二中择一；adj. 选择性的，二中择一的
arbitrary [ʹɑːbitrəri] adj. 任意的
collinear [kəʹlinjə] adj. 共线的，在同一直线上的
component [kəmʹpəunənt] n. 成分，元件，组件
concurrent [kənʹkʌrənt] adj. 同时发生的，一致的
constraint [kənʹstreint] n. 强制，约束
deduce [diʹdjuːs] vt. 推论，推断，演绎(from)；引出，推导
dimension [diʹmenʃən] n. 尺寸，维数，大小
eliminate [iʹlimineit] vt. 消除，排除
equate [iʹkweit] vt. 使相等；vi. 等同
equilibrium [ˌiːkwiʹlibriəm] n. 平衡，均衡
equivalent [iʹkwivələnt] adj. 相等的，相当的，等价的；n. 等价物，相等物
exert [igʹzəːt] vt. 施加(力)；行使，尽力，施行
impose [imʹpəuz] vt. 把…强加于；vi. 利用，欺骗，施加影响
interaction [ˌintərʹækʃən] n. 交互作用；相互作用，相互影响；干扰
isolate [ʹaisəleit] vt. 使隔离，使绝缘
moment [ʹməumənt] n. 力矩，片刻，瞬间
parameter [pəʹræmitə] n. 参量，参数
perpendicular [ˌpəːpənʹdikjulə] adj. 垂直的，正交的；n. 垂线
react [riʹækt] vi. 起反应，起作用
reaction [ri(ː)ʹækʃən] n. 反应
replace [ri(ː)ʹpleis] vt. 替换，代替，取代
resultant [riʹzʌltənt] n. 合力；adj. 合成的
rigid [ʹridʒid] adj. 刚性的，坚硬的，严格的
scalar [ʹskeilə] n. 数量，标量；adj. 数量的，标量的

tendency ['tendənsi] *n.* 趋向,倾向
trivial ['triviəl] *adj.* 琐碎的,不重要的
visualize ['vizjuəlaiz,'viʒ-] *vt.* 想象,形象化,使看得见;
　　　　　　　　　　　　　vi. 显形,显现

Lesson 7

Newton's Laws of Motion

1. Everyday experience leads one to the conclusion that the cause of motion is force. Children playing with wooden trains or wheeled animals soon find out for themselves that pulling the string attached to the toy will cause the toy to move. In order to move the toy in several different directions it is necessary to push or pull in those different directions. Thus each force has associated with it a given direction. Similarly, each force has associated with it a magnitude-the child can push or pull the toy harder in order to obtain a more positive result.

2. An investigation of dynamics requires a quantified description of motion. Three fundamental kinematical quantities used to describe the motion of a particle are position, velocity, and acceleration. These basic terms are defined with respect to a frame of reference that describes the three-dimensional space within which the motion occurs.

3. In most situations, the motion of the earth is negligible in comparison to the motion of the object of interest. The reference frame in such cases may be considered to be attached to the earth. To describe the motion of a particle we must postulate that the reference frame is fixed, that is, stationary, in space. Although considering the earth to be fixed is not

exactly correct, the errors that result from this assumption are negligible for most systems. This reference frame can be visualized as a set of rectangular Cartesian axes xyz.

4. The laws of motion stated by Sir Isaac Newton (1642 ~ 1727) in his historic work Principia (1687) are the foundation of the study of dynamics. The simplest possible motion to discuss is that of a particle moving under the influence of no force. Such a particle is said to be moving freely, and its motion is governed by Newton's first law of motion, i.e.,

FIRST LAW: *A particle will remain at rest or move with constant speed along a straight line, unless it is acted upon by a resultant force.*

5. The magnitude and direction of a given force acting on a given particle can be modeled together as a vector, say F, which will intuitively cause the particle to move. What property of the motion is related to the force? Intuition would certainly lead most readers to argue that the larger the force the faster the particle moves and so to relate the velocity of the particle to the force acting on the particle. This was the common mistake made by mathematicians in the pre-Newtonian era - a mistake which prevented significant progress in mechanics for many years. It is known that the velocity of a particle varies from one reference frame to another. Hence if the velocity is related to the force, the relationship could only hold in one particular reference frame.

6. Unlike velocity, the acceleration of a particle is independent of the reference frame relative to which the acceleration is measured, and so if the acceleration of the particle were related to the force acting on the particle then the

relationship would hold in all reference frames rather than in only one particular reference frame. This relationship was in fact postulated by Newton and is incorporated in his second law of motion, i.e.,

SECOND LAW: *When a resultant force is exerted on a particle, the acceleration of that particle is parallel to the direction of the force and the magnitude of the acceleration is proportional to the magnitude of the force.*

If a particle P of mass m is moving with acceleration a under the action of a force F then according to Newton's second law of motion,

$$ma = F \qquad (1)$$

7. Newton's second law involves the force acting on the particle. In most cases several different forces will be acting on the particle simultaneously, and it is therefore necessary to postulate that it is the vector sum of all the individual forces which must be used as the force in applying the second law. This postulate is in agreement with the concept of the resultant of several forces in statics, and the necessity for making such a postulate was first realized by Mach in 1883.

8. Newton's third law of motion can be stated as follows.

THIRD LAW: *The force exerted on one particle by another is equal and opposite to the force exerted by the first particle on the second.*

In fact, most forces between particles obey the third law of motion and such forces are sometimes called Newtonian.

New Words and Expressions

acceleration [æk͵selə'reiʃən] n. 加速度
argue ['ɑ:gju:] vi. 争论, 辩论; vt. 说服
associate [ə'souʃieit] vt. 联合, 结交, 使发生联系; vi. 结交, 联合; n. 伴侣
assumption [ə'sʌmpʃən] n. 假定
dynamics [dai'næmiks] n. 动力学
frame [freim] n. 框架, 结构
independent [indi'pendənt] adj. 独立的, 不须依赖的
intuitive [in'tju(:)itiv] adj. 直觉的, 直观的
intuitively adv. 直觉地, 直观地
involve [in'vɔlv] vt. 包括, 包含, 包围; 潜心于, 使陷于
kinematic [͵kaini'mætik] adj. 运动学的, 运动学上的
kinematical adj. 运动学的
negligible ['neglidʒəbl] adj. 可以忽略的, 微不足道的
particle ['pɑ:tikl] n. 质点, 颗粒, 粒子
postulate ['pɔstjuleit] n. 假定, 先决[必要]条件; v. 假定, 假设
rectangular [rek'tæŋgjulə] adj. 矩形的, 成直角的
simultaneous [͵siməl'teinjəs] adj. 同时的, 同时发生
stationary ['steiʃ(ə)nəri] adj. 不动的, 稳定的, 定常的
string [striŋ] n. 线, 细绳
vector ['vektə] n. 矢量
velocity [vi'lɔsiti] n. 速度

Lesson 8

The Planar Motion of A Rigid Body

1. The planar motion of a rigid body occurs when the path of each point lies wholly in a plane, with the planar paths for all points in the body being parallel to each other. A simple example is a wheel mounted on a rotating shaft. The plane of the motion of any point in that system is perpendicular to the axis of the shaft. The restriction to planar motion substantially simplifies the kinematical description in comparison to a general three-dimensional motion. One of the attributes of this simplification is that it will be possible to depict the motion by means of a planar diagram. Without loss of generality, we will always let the xy plane coincide with the plane of motion.

2. By definition, a rigid body is a system of particles that are always at a fixed distance from each other. This geometric restriction means that the movement of any point in the body relative to any other is limited. The existence of such kinematical relations is contrasted by the situation where particles in a system are not rigidly connected. All materials deform when forces are applied to them. The concept of a rigid body is merely a model that we create as an approximation. When we use the rigid body model, we are assuming that the movement of points due to deformation is negligible.

3. Let us consider three arbitrarily selected points A, B and C to be scribed onto a body. The triangle ABC depicted in Figure 1 is useful for characterizing the kinematics of a rigid body motion. To describe where the triangle ABC is situated in space, it would be sufficient to know the coordinates (x_A, y_A) locating point A, and the angle ϕ between the x axis and side AB. From this information, the position of a rigid body at any instant is defined by the absolute position of a point in the body and the angular orientation of any line in the body.

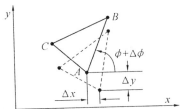

Fig.1 The rigid body motion

4. Our knowledge of the information required to locate the position of a rigid body permits us to describe how the position changes with time. Figure 1 depicts the position of triangle ABC at an instant subsequent to the original position of the triangle indicated by the dashed lines. The distances Δx_A and Δy_A describe the movement of point A, and $\Delta \phi$ describes the angle of rotation of line AB. By the definition of a rigid body we know that the angles between all sides of the triangle are constant. It follows then that each line undergoes the same rotation. Hence, angular motion is an overall property of the motion of the body. It is the same regardless of which points in the body are being discussed.

5. Now, suppose that the movement of point A is specified.

In addition to this movement, points B and C may move relative to point A. Because the angular motion is an overall property, the radial lines from point A to points B and C undergo the same rotation. In other words, each point moves in a circular path relative to point A. Therefore, we may conclude that

> *The motion of a rigid body consists of a superposition of two movements. The first part consists of a movement of all points following the motion of an arbitrarily selected point in the body. The second movement is a rotation about the selected point in which all lines rotate by the same amount.*

This statement is known as Chasle's theorem.

6. Special terms are used to describe the motion of rigid bodies. One simple type of motion occurs when every line in the body retains its original orientation, that is, there is no rotation. This is called a translation. Another simple type of motion occurs when one point in the body is fixed in space. Chasle's theorem states that the motion of the body may be considered to consist solely of a rotation about the fixed point, this is called a pure rotation. Chasle's theorem may be reworded to state that the motion of a rigid body is the superposition of a translation of an arbitrary point and a pure rotation about that point.

7. Suppose that the motion of point A in the rigid body shown in Figure 2 is known, as is the angular rotation of the body, ω. Point B is an arbitrarily chosen point whose motion we seek. As shown in Figure 2 the vectors r_{AO} and r_{BO} denote the positions of points A and B respectively. Note that ω is

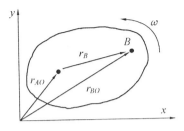

Fig. 2 The position vectors

independent of the choice for points A and B, because Chasle's theorem states that the rotation is the same for all lines in a rigid body. The absolute value of ω is called the angular speed of the rigid body.

8. The qualitative insight provided by Chasle's theorem will enable us to form algebraic relations for determining the velocities and accelerations of points on a rigid body. The relationship between the absolute motions of points A and B is readily formed by referring to the position vectors depicted in figure 2, i.e.,

$$\overline{r}_{BO} = \overline{r}_{AO} + \overline{r}_{BA} \tag{1}$$

$$\overline{v}_B = \overline{v}_A + \overline{v}_{BA} = \overline{v}_A + \overline{\omega} \times \overline{r}_{BA} \tag{2}$$

$$\overline{a}_B = \overline{a}_A + \overline{a}_{BA} = \overline{a}_A + \overline{\alpha} \times \overline{r}_{BA} - \omega^2 \overline{r}_{BA} \tag{3}$$

In the above equations (2) and (3), the velocity and acceleration of point A are denoted by $\overline{v}_A$ and $\overline{a}_A$ respectively. The symbols $\overline{v}_B$ and $\overline{a}_B$ are similarly defined for point B. The vector $\overline{\omega}$ is the angular velocity of the body, and $\overline{\alpha}$ is the angular acceleration. Both vectors are perpendicular to the plane of motion, so they are parallel to the axis for the rotational portion of the motion. As usual, the angular unit for $\overline{\omega}$ and $\overline{\alpha}$ must be radians.

New Words and Expressions

acceleration [æk͵selə'reiʃən] n. 加速度
angular ['æŋgjulə] adj. 角的，角度的
approximation [ə͵prɔksi'meiʃən] n. 接近，近似值
attribute [ə'tribju(:)t] n. 属性,特质; vt. 把…归因于(to)…
characterize ['kæriktəraiz] vt. 描绘,刻画;描绘…的特性，表…特点;具有…特征
coincide [͵kəuin'said] vi. 一致，符合
contrast ['kɔntræst] n. 对比; vt. 使对比
coordinate [kəu'ɔ:dinit] n. 坐标
deform [di'fɔ:m] vt. 使变形; vi. 变形
depict [di'pikt] vt. 描述，描写，描绘，叙述
dimensional [di'menʃənəl] adj. 尺寸的,空间的;有量纲的; …维的,…度空间的
kinematics [͵kaini'mætiks] n. 运动学
orientation [͵ɔ(:)rien'teiʃən] n. 方向，定方位
parallel ['pærəlel] n. 平行; adj. 平行的
particle ['pɑ:tikl] n. 颗粒，质点
perpendicular [͵pə:pən'dikjulə] n. 垂直线; adj. 垂直的
planar ['pleinə] adj. 平面的
radial ['reidjəl] adj. 径向的
radian ['reidjən] n. 弧度
restriction [ris'trikʃən] n. 限制，约束
retain [ri'tein] vt. 保持，留住
rigid ['ridʒid] adj. 刚性的，严格的
scribe [skraib] vt. 用划线器划，划痕
shaft [ʃɑ:ft] n. 轴
subsequent ['sʌbsikwənt] adj. 接下去的,后来的,随[其]后的,其次的

substantially [səb'stænʃ(ə)li] *adv.* 主要地,实质上地
superposition [ˌsjuːpəpə'ziʃən] *n.* 重叠,重合
symbol ['simbəl] *n.* 符号
vector ['vektə] *n.* 矢量
velocity [vi'lɔsiti] *n.* 速度

Lesson 9

Theorems of Particle Dynamics

1. In solving many problems of dynamics it will be found that the general theorems of particle dynamics are more conveniently applied than the method of integration of differential equations of motion. The importance of the general theorems is that they establish visual relationships between the principal dynamic characteristics of motion of material bodies, thereby presenting broad possibilities for analyzing the mechanical motions widely employed in practical engineering. Furthermore, the general theorems make it possible to study for practical purposes the specific aspects of a given phenomenon without investigating the phenomenon as a whole. Now let us see how these theorems apply to one material particle.

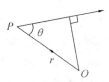

Fig.1 The position vector r of particle P

2. The vector approach will now be used in order that the motion may be discussed without the introduction of a specific coordinate system. As shown in Figure 1, a particle P is located

at the point with position vector r relative to a given origin o. The velocity and acceleration of the particle relative to o are $v = \dot{r}$ and $a = \ddot{r}$ respectively. If the particle is of mass m and is moving under the action of a force F then Newton's second law of motion leads to the equation of motion as follows,

$$M\ddot{r} = F \tag{1}$$

If more than one force is acting on the particle, then F is the vector sum of all the individual forces.

3. It will always be assumed that the mass m of a particle is a constant. This means that Eq. (1) can be expressed by the following equation,

$$\frac{\mathrm{d}}{\mathrm{d}t}(mv) = F \tag{2}$$

The vector mv is defined to be the linear momentum of the particle. Eq. (2) shows that the rate of change of the linear momentum is equal to the total force acting on the particle. If the total force F acting on a given particle is zero then it follows from Eq. (2) that the linear momentum mv is a constant. The linear momentum is said to be conserved and the equation

$$mv = \text{constant}$$

is called the equation of conservation of linear momentum.

4. Let a particle of mass m moving under the action of a force F have a velocity v_0 at time $t = t_0$, and at time t_1 let its velocity be v_1. Now multiply both sides of Eq. (2) by $\mathrm{d}t$ and take definite integrals, we have

$$mv_1 - mv_0 = \int_{t_0}^{t_1} F \mathrm{d}t \tag{3}$$

As shown in Eq. (3), the integral on the right side is the impulse of the acting force during a certain interval of time. In words, Eq.

(3) states that the change in the linear momentum equals the linear impulse.

5. Often, in analyzing the motion of a particle, it is necessary to consider the change not in the vector mv itself but in its moment. Taking the vector product of Eq. (2) with r gives

$$r \times \frac{\mathrm{d}}{\mathrm{d}t}(mv) = r \times F \qquad (4)$$

Since $\mathrm{d}r/\mathrm{d}t = v$, and $\mathrm{d}r/\mathrm{d}t \times mv = 0$, after simple manipulations, Eq. (4) can be rewritten as

$$\frac{\mathrm{d}}{\mathrm{d}t}(r \times mv) = r \times F \qquad (5)$$

The expression $r \times mv$ is called the moment of the linear momentum or angular momentum of the particle about point o. Eq. (5) shows that the rate of change of the angular momentum of the particle about o is equal to the moment about o of the total force acting on the particle. If the moment $r \times F$ is zero, then we have

$$r \times mv = \text{constant}$$

that is the equation of conservation of angular momentum about point o.

6. Now consider a particle which travels from a point with position vector r to another point with position vector $r + \delta r$ under the action of a non-constant force F. The force will remain almost constant and so the infinitesimal amount of work δw done by this force will be defined by $\delta w = F \cdot \delta r$. The total work done by the force in moving the particle from some fixed position r_0 to its current position r is therefore defined as

$$W = \int_{r_0}^{r} F \cdot \mathrm{d}r \qquad (6)$$

In general, the value of this integral will depend upon the path which the particle takes in moving from r_0 to r. If in fact the integral is independent of the path, then the force F is defined to be conservative. For such a force, the integral will define a unique function of position.

7. For any vector v, $\mathrm{d}v^2/\mathrm{d}t = \mathrm{d}(v \cdot v)/\mathrm{d}t = 2v \cdot \mathrm{d}v/\mathrm{d}t$, substituting $F = m\ddot{r}$ into Eq.(6), and according to the chain rule for differentiation the above equation for the work then becomes

$$W = \frac{1}{2}m(v_2^2 - v_1^2) \qquad (7)$$

The quantity $\frac{1}{2}mv^2$ is defined to be the kinetic energy of the particle. In words, the work done by the forces acting on a particle is the amount by which the kinetic energy of the particle changes from the initial to the final position.

New Words and Expressions

acceleration [ækˌselə'reiʃən] n. 加速度
angular ['æŋgjulə] adj. 有角的，角度的
characterization [ˌkæriktərai'zeiʃən] n. 特征，特性
conservation [ˌkɔnsə(ː)'veiʃən] n. 守恒，保存
conservative [kən'sɔːvətiv] adj. 保守的，有保存力的
conserve [kən'sɔːv] v. 使(能量等)守恒，保存
coordinate [kəu'ɔːdinit] n. 坐标
differential [ˌdifə'renʃəl] adj. 微分的，差别的
differentiation [ˌdifəˌrenʃi'eiʃən] n. 微分
dynamics [dai'næmiks] n. 动力学
equation [i'kweiʃən] n. 方程，等式
impulse ['impʌls] n. 脉冲，冲力，冲动
infinitesimal [ˌinˌfini'tesiməl] adj. 无限小的；n. 无限小量

integral ['intigrəl] adj. 积分的,整体的
integrate ['intigreit] vt. 积分,综合,集成,使一体化; v. 结合
integration [ˌinti'greiʃən] n. 积分,集成,一体化
interval ['intəvəl] n. 间隔,间隙,空隙
kinetic [kai'netik] adj. 运动的,活动的
linear ['liniə] adj. 直线的,线性的,一次的
manipulation [məˌnipju'leiʃən] n. 操作,处理
moment ['məumənt] n. 力矩,瞬间,片刻
momentum [məu'mentəm] n. 动量,动力
particle ['pɑ:tikl] n. 颗粒,质点
phenomenon [fi'nɔminən] n. 现象,迹象
theorem ['θiərəm] n. 定理,法则
vector ['vektə] n. 矢量
velocity [vi'lɔsiti] n. 速度

Lesson 10

Vibrations of A Single Particle

1. When a medium is disturbed by the passage of a wave through it, the particles comprising the medium are caused to vibrate. To take a simple example, corks floating on the surface of a pond will bob up and down owing to the influence of water waves. The bob of a simple pendulum and the weight hanging freely from the end of a spring are other examples of particles which may be set in vibration, and most readers will have a good mental picture of how these vibrate.

2. The motion of a vibrating particle is periodic, that is, after equal intervals of time (the period T) the system finds itself in exactly the same situation. The bob of the pendulum, for example, is found to be at the same position, moving with the same velocity and acceleration as it was T seconds earlier, and these quantities will be the same T, $2T$, $3T$, etc. seconds later. During the interval of one period, a vibrating system is said to go through a cycle of situations, and the frequency (f) is defined as the number of cycles occurring in one second. Clearly, then, $f = 1/T$, the dimension of f is $second^{-1}$. This unit is termed the hertz (Hz).

3. The simplest kind of periodic motion is that experienced by a point, moving along a straight line, whose acceleration is

directed towards a fixed point on the line and is proportional to its distance from the fixed point. This is called simple harmonic motion (s.h.m.). Suppose a point P moves along a straight line so that its position with respect to a fixed point o is completely specified by the single coordinate x. The acceleration of the moving point is d^2x/dt^2, which is directed towards the point o and proportional to the distance x. Thus

$$d^2x/dt^2 + \omega^2 x = 0 \qquad (1)$$

where ω is a positive constant.

4. Equation (1) shown above is a linear, second-order differential equation. The word linear is due to x and its derivative appear to the power one only, and second order because the highest derivative is d^2x/dt^2. Equation (1) is referred to as the differential equation governing the motion. It is not the equation of motion. To find the equation of motion we have to solve Eq.(1) for x and obtain the general solution as follows

$$x = a\sin(\omega t + \varepsilon) \qquad (2)$$

The quantity $\omega t + \varepsilon$ is known as the phase of the motion and ε the phase constant or epoch. The constant a is the amplitude of the motion. It is the greatest possible value that x can have, since the maximum value of $\sin(\omega t + \varepsilon)$ is unit. Thus the motion takes place entirely between the limits $x = \pm a$.

5. The vibrating systems we considered above vibrated for ever with undiminished amplitude. Real physical systems do not, of course, vibrate indefinitely. For example, oscillation of a mass suspended on an elastic string eventually comes to rest. The reason for the decay is that the energy originally stored in the system is gradually transformed into heat energy by a number of processes. The suspended mass, as it moves, experiences a

viscous force due to the air through which it passes. Work has to be done to overcome this force, and hence energy is lost. Even if the mass were in vacuum, there would be hysteresis losses in stretching the elastic string, and also frictional losses where the fixed end of the string is clamped.

6. It is an experimental fact that when a particle moves through a viscous fluid, such as a gas, there is a resistive force which is proportional to the velocity of the particle relative to the fluid, provided the velocity is not too great. Frictional forces can also be shown experimentally to be proportional to relative velocity. The resultant of all the forces which resist the motion may be regarded as a single damping force.

7. Further, we will assume that this force at any instant is proportional to the particle velocity, i.e., the damping force is equal to $D\ dx/dt$, where D is the coefficient of damping. Applying Newton's second law of motion to the particle of mass m gives

$$m d^2 x/dt^2 + D dx/dt + kx = 0 \qquad (3)$$

The actual equation of motion can be obtained by solving this differential equation. It is shown that the behavior of solution x as a function of t depends on the magnitude of the damping constant.

8. The vibrating systems treated in the preceding sections are sometimes referred to as free vibrations. The frequency of such vibrations is entirely determined by the system itself. There is no further interference by the outside world, in particular no further energy is introduced. When a vibrating system is subjected to a continuous periodic disturbance of some kind, the resulting vibrations are known as forced vibrations which are quite different from free vibrations.

9. Let us consider the simplest case of vibration where a mass m suspended from an elastic string of stiffness k is subjected to a varying force. The force has maximum value F_0 and varies sinusoidally with time. When we include the driving force in Eq. (3), we obtain, by a direct application of Newton's second law of motion

$$m\mathrm{d}^2x/\mathrm{d}t^2 + D\mathrm{d}x/\mathrm{d}t + kx = F_0\sin pt \qquad (4)$$

This is the differential equation of damped forced vibration of a particle. The quantity p in Eq.(4) is called the circular frequency.

10. From the theory of differential equation, the solution of Eq.(4) is $x = x_1 + x_2$, where x_1 is the general solution of the equation without the right side, and x_2 is a particular solution of the complete equation. The contribution of the general solution x_1 diminishes with time, for which reason it is called the transient solution. On the other hand, the particular solution x_2 does not vanish for large t and is known as the steady-state solution. Thus the transient and steady-state solutions can be obtained separately and then combined to obtain the complete solution.

New Words and Expressions

amplitude ['æmplitjuːd] $n.$ 幅度,振幅,充足,丰富
clamp [klæmp] $vt.$ 夹紧,夹住
cork [kɔːk] $n.$ 软木塞
cycle ['saikl] $n.$ 周期,循环
damp [dæmp] $vt.$ 使阻尼; $vi.$ 衰减
decay [di'kei] $n.$ 衰退,衰减; $vi.$ 衰减,衰落,腐朽,腐烂
derivative [di'rivətiv] $n.$ 导数; $adj.$ 派生的
differential [ˌdifə'renʃəl] $adj.$ 微分的; $n.$ 微分
diminish [di'miniʃ] $v.$ (使)减少,(使)变小

disturb [dis'tə:b] vt. 扰乱,扰动,干涉
epoch ['i:pɔk,'epɔk] n. 新纪元,时代,时期
frequency ['fri:kwənsi] n. 频率
friction ['frikʃən] n. 摩擦
harmonic [hɑ:'mɔnik] adj. 和谐的,和声的,融洽的; n. 谐波,和声,谐函数
hertz ['hə:ts] n. 赫兹
hysteresis [ˌhistə'ri:sis] n. 滞后,迟滞性
interference [ˌintə'fiərəns] n. 干涉,干扰
interval ['intəvəl] n. 间隔,间距
magnitude ['mægnitju:d] n. 大小,量级
oscillation [ˌɔsi'leiʃən] n. 振动,摆动
pendulum ['pendjuləm] n. 钟摆,摇锤
period ['piəriəd] n. 周期,循环,时期,时代,期间
periodic [piəri'ɔdik] adj. 周期(性)的,定期的,循环的
phase [feiz] n. 位相,阶段
power ['pauə] n. 力量,乘方,幂
preceding [pri(:)'si:diŋ] adj. 前面的,上述的
resultant [ri'zʌltənt] adj. 合成的; n. 合力
separate ['sepəreit] adj. 分开的,分离的; vt. 使分离,隔离,分散,分别
sinusoidal [ˌsainə'sɔidəl] adj. 正弦(波,曲线)的
suspend [səs'pend] vt. 吊,悬挂,使悬浮; v. 延缓
transient ['trænziənt] adj. 瞬变的,短暂的,瞬时的; n. 瞬态,瞬变(过程,现象,函数)
vanish ['væniʃ] vi. 消失,成为零
vibration [vai'breiʃən] n. 振动
viscous ['viskəs] adj. 粘性的
wave [weiv] n. 波,波动

Lesson 11

Stress Equilibrium and Compatibility

1. When a body is subjected to the actions of external forces, the effects are transmitted through the material. Internal forces are thus induced with the result that the material on one side of any section of the body will in general exert a force on the material on the other side. In considering the transmission of force through a body, one must be concerned not only with resultant forces but also with the distribution of the force. In order to do this it is necessary to define a quantity which describes the intensity of a distributed force at a point. This quantity is known as the stress.

2. In order to define the stress components at a point in a solid, one must make reference to a surface through the point. The direction chosen for this reference surface is arbitrary and in fact it is necessary to give the stress components on at least three surfaces in order to completely describe the state of stress at the point. By convention the three surfaces chosen as reference surfaces are taken perpendicular to the three coordinate axes x_1, x_2, and x_3 respectively.

3. The state of stress at the center of a small rectangular parallelepiped element with surfaces perpendicular to the coordinate axes is defined as the limiting value of the ratio F_{ij}/A_i, where A_i is the area of the surface on which the resultant force

component F_{ij} acts. Since there are three stress components on each of the three faces of the element, there are nine stress components in all.

4. Since stresses are related to the resultant forces acting on surfaces within bodies, the laws of mechanics can be used to derive the condition of equilibrium. Just as $F = ma$ must hold for the entire body, it must also hold for a small element of the body. The resultant forces and moments acting on this body can be expressed in terms of the stress components acting on each of the faces and the area of the face. If in addition to the stresses there is also a force per unit volume which acts on the body, such as gravitational, electrostatic, or magnetic attraction, there can be an additional resultant force acting on the body. This force is called the body force.

5. Since it is necessary that the resultant force acting on the element in each of the coordinate directions must be equal to the mass of the element times its acceleration a_i in that direction, one may write for the x_i direction

$$\frac{\partial \sigma_{11}}{\partial x_1} + \frac{\partial \sigma_{21}}{\partial x_2} + \frac{\partial \sigma_{31}}{\partial x_3} + X_i = \rho a_1 \qquad (1)$$

where X_i is the body force component and ρ is the mass density of the body. Similar equations are obtained by summing forces in the x_2 and x_3 directions.

6. The element must also obey the condition that the resultant torque must be equal to the rate of change of angular momentum. Since the moment of inertia becomes zero in the limit as the dimensions of the element go to zero, this condition implies that the resultant torques must vanish. So one obtains

$$\sigma_{12} = \sigma_{21} \qquad \sigma_{23} = \sigma_{32} \qquad \sigma_{31} = \sigma_{13} \qquad (2)$$

It should be emphasized that these equations of equilibrium are simply a specific expression of Newton's Second Law. These equations therefore hold for all materials regardless of the type of material behavior involved.

7. In addition to describing the stresses in a body, problems in continuum mechanics also require the description of the deformation of the body. The deformation of the body can be completely described by giving the displacement of each point in the body from its undeformed position to its deformed position. However, for many applications it is more convenient to use the linear elastic strains defined in terms of the derivatives of the displacements, that is $\varepsilon_{ij} = \frac{1}{2}(\partial u_i/\partial x_j + \partial u_j/\partial x_i)$, where u_i is the displacement component in the x direction. The linear expressions used above are descriptions of the internal changes in the structure of the body only when the displacements u_i are sufficiently small that the second-order terms can be neglected.

8. Since six strain components are derived from three displacement components, it is clear that the strain components are not all independent quantities. That is, one may not say that any arbitrary set of six functions are the components of strain in a body. Additional restrictions must be placed on the functions to ensure that the strains can be integrated to give a displacement field which is single valued and independent of the path of integration. These conditions are called compatibility conditions. These compatibility conditions ensure that if one were to divide the body up into small elements and deform each element according to the local value of the strain, he could then reassemble the elements into a complete body with no holes or overlapping

material.

9. In mathematical formulations of continuum mechanics, the compatibility conditions are expressed as a series of second-order partial differential equations. These equations can be written as

$$\frac{\partial^2 \varepsilon_{11}}{\partial x_2^2} + \frac{\partial^2 \varepsilon_{22}}{\partial x_1^2} = \frac{\partial^2 \varepsilon_{12}}{\partial x_1 \partial x_2} \qquad (3)$$

$$\frac{2\partial^2 \varepsilon_{11}}{\partial x_2 \partial x_3} = \frac{\partial}{\partial x_1}\left(\frac{\partial \varepsilon_{12}}{\partial x_3} - \frac{\partial \varepsilon_{23}}{\partial x_1} + \frac{\partial \varepsilon_{31}}{\partial x_2}\right) \qquad (4)$$

Two other equations similar to each of equations (3) and (4) can be written down by cyclic permutation. These six equations are known as the equations of compatibility and must be satisfied by the solution of any general three-dimensional problem. The equations of compatibility may also be expressed in terms of stresses instead of strains by using appropriate stress-strain relations.

10. As in the case of stress equilibrium, it has not been necessary to state anything about the material in question. It is therefore clear that the equations of compatibility are once again universal and must be satisfied for all bodies independent of the nature of mechanical behavior of the material involved.

New Words and Expressions

acceleration [æk₁selə'reiʃən] n. 加速度，促进
angular ['æŋgjulə] adj. 角的，角度的
compatibility [kəm₁pæti'biliti] n. 相容性,兼容性
continuum [kən'tinjuəm] n. 连续体,连续统
cyclic ['saiklik] adj. 周期的,循环的
deformation [₁di:fɔ:'meiʃən] n. 变形,畸形
density ['densiti] n. 密度，浓度，比重

derivative [di'rivətiv] *adj.* 引出的,派生的 *n.* 派生物,导数
differential [ˌdifə'renʃəl] *adj.* 微分的,差别的
displacement [dis'pleismənt] *n.* 位移,移动,换置
electrostatic [i'lektrəu'stætik] *adj.* 静电的,静电学的
element ['elimənt] *n.* 元素,元件,要素,成分,组成部分,分子
equilibrium [ˌi:kwi'libriəm] *n.* 平衡,均衡
exert [ig'zə:t] *vt.* 运用,施加,尽(力); *vi.* 发挥,尽
gravitation [ˌɡrævi'teiʃn] *n.* 重力,引力,地心吸力
gravitational *adj.* 重力的
induce [in'dju:s] *vt.* 招致,导致,引起,感应,归纳出
inertia [i'nə:ʃjə] *n.* 惯性,惰性
integrate ['intiɡreit] *vt.* 使成整体,使一体化,求…的积分; *v.* 结合,集成
intensity [in'tensiti] *n.* 强度,强烈,亮度
magnetic [mæɡ'netik] *adj.* 磁性的,有吸引力的
moment ['məumənt] *n.* 力矩,瞬间
momentum [məu'mentəm] *n.* 动量,动力
overlap ['əuvə'læp] *vt.* 与……交搭,叠盖住; *vi.* 重叠,交搭,叠盖
parallelepiped [ˌpærəle'lepiped] *n.* 平行六面体
partial ['pɑ:ʃəl] *adj.* 部分的,偏的,偏微分的
permutation [ˌpə:mju(:)'teiʃən] *n.* 交换,置换,更动
perpendicular [ˌpə:pən'dikjulə] *adj.* 垂直的,正交的; *n.* 垂线
reassemble ['ri:ə'sembl] *vt.* 重新召集,重新装配; *vi.* 重新集合
rectangular [rek'tæŋɡjulə] *adj.* 矩形的,成直角的
restriction [ris'trikʃən] *n.* 限制,约束
resultant [ri'zʌltənt] *adj.* 合成的; *n.* 合力,合量
torque [tɔ:k] *n.* 扭转力,扭矩
vanish ['væniʃ] *vi.* 消失,成为零

Lesson 12

Elastic Constitutive Relations

1. If the equations of equilibrium and compatibility are examined, it is found that the equations which involve stresses involve only stresses, body forces, and accelerations, but do not involve strains or displacements. Furthermore, those equations which involve strains and displacements do not contain stresses.

2. Since the application of forces to a body produces both stress and deformation, it is expected that the stresses on an element can be related to the deformation which these stresses produce. Such a set of relationships will then complete the description of the action of loads on the body. Experience has demonstrated that these relationships will depend on the material in question.

3. For most engineering materials, elastic strains are always sufficiently small that the relationship between the stresses and strains is linear. The most general set of linear relations which could be written is

$$\sigma_{ij} = \sum_{k=1}^{3} \sum_{l=1}^{3} C_{ijkl} \varepsilon_{kl} \qquad (1)$$

The C_{ijkl}'s are proportionality constants, where i and j can have any value from 1 to 3. The number of constants C_{ijkl} required is therefore $3^4 = 81$. From equilibrium it is known that $\sigma_{ij} = \sigma_{ji}$ and by definition $\varepsilon_{ij} = \varepsilon_{ji}$.

4. From energy arguments it can be shown that $C_{ijkl} = C_{klij}$. These conditions combined imply that the number of independent constants which must be specified in the most general linear elastic formulation is 21. Since materials generally have a great deal of symmetry, arguments based on the equivalence of various directions in a material can be used to further reduce the number of constants required.

5. For an isotropic material, one in which all directions are equivalent, it can be shown that the material has only two independent elastic constants and a great many zeros in the general formulation above. Hence, it is convenient to rewrite the general equation above in the more familiar form of Hooke's law:

$$\varepsilon_{11} = \frac{1}{E}[\sigma_{11} - v(\sigma_{22} + \sigma_{33})] \quad \text{etc.} \quad (2a)$$

$$\varepsilon_{12} = \frac{\sigma_{12}}{2G} \quad \text{etc.} \quad (2b)$$

6. As was stated above, only two of the three constants represented by the symbols E, v, and G can be independent. It can be shown that

$$G = \frac{E}{2(1 + v)} \quad (3)$$

When the constants E and G are specified, the six equations of Eqs. (2a, b) form the link between the stress and the strain relations of continuum mechanics.

7. Another formulation which will prove useful in relating elastic behavior to other types of material behavior separates the volume change portion of the strain from the distortional portion. For any state of strain, the change in volume per unit volume $(\Delta v/v)$ is the sum of the three normal strain components, that is

$$\Delta v/v = I_1 = \varepsilon = \varepsilon_{11} + \varepsilon_{22} + \varepsilon_{33} \tag{4}$$

The symbol I_1 is used to denote the first strain invariant. So we have

$$[\varepsilon_{ij}] = [\varepsilon'_{ij}] + \frac{\varepsilon}{3}[I] \tag{5}$$

where $[I]$ is a 3×3 unit matrix. The first matrix on the right-hand side represents a state of strain for which the volume change is zero, while the second matrix represents a pure change in volume with no distortion.

8. The state of strain represented by the second matrix will be called the dilatation strain. The terms of the first matrix on the right-hand side are called deviator strain components and they are denoted by the symbol ε'_{ij} defined by

$$\varepsilon'_{ij} = \varepsilon_{ij} - \delta_{ij}\frac{\varepsilon}{3} \tag{6}$$

where the symbol δ_{ij} is called the Kronecker delta.

9. A state of stress may be similarly decomposed into deviator and hydrostatic components. The hydrostatic or mean normal stress is defined as

$$\sigma = \frac{1}{3}J_1 = \frac{1}{3}(\sigma_{11} + \sigma_{22} + \sigma_{33}) \tag{7}$$

where J_1 is the first invariant of the stress tensor. A state of stress can then be decomposed into the deviator stress and the hydrostatic stress.

$$[\sigma_{ij}] = [\sigma'_{ij}] + \sigma[I] \tag{8}$$

The second matrix on the right-hand side is called the hydrostatic stress, which is the same in all directions. The first matrix on the right-hand side is the deviator stress, which is a state of stress with zero hydrostatic component. The deviator stress components are therefore defined as

$$\sigma'_{ij} = \sigma_{ij} - \delta_{ij}\sigma \tag{9}$$

10. In an isotropic elastic body, a state of stress with a zero hydrostatic component produces only distortion and no volume change in the body. A purely hydrostatic state of stress produces only a volume change with no distortion. Hooke's law, expressed in terms of the decomposed stresses and strains, is

$$\varepsilon'_{ij} = \frac{\sigma'_{ij}}{2G}, \qquad \varepsilon = \frac{\sigma}{B} \tag{10}$$

where B is the bulk modulus, i.e., $B = E/3(1 - 2v)$. Notice that in Eq. (10) the form of the deviator stress-deviator strain relationship is the same for all components, and that the dilatation strain is a function of only the hydrostatic stress.

11. The elastic constitutive relations, the equilibrium equations, and the compatibility conditions form a complete description of the behavior of linearly elastic materials under the action of loads. Since the number of those equations equals the number of unknown quantities, it is possible, in principle, to determine the distribution of stress in a body when the distribution of tractions on the surface is given. In practice, however, the solution of a boundary value problem in three dimensions is a nearly impossible task. The methods which involve various approximate mathematical techniques have been shown to be most successful in generating solutions of many engineering problems.

New Words and Expressions

acceleration [ækˌseləˈreiʃən] $n.$ 加速度
argument [ˈɑːgjumənt] $n.$ 论证,论点,自变量
bulk [bʌlk] $n.$ 大块,体积

compatibility [kəmˌpæti'biliti] n. 相容性；兼容性
constitutive ['kɔnstitjuːtiv] adj. 构成的，本构的，制定的
continuum [kən'tinjuəm] n. 连续体，连续统一体
decompose [ˌdiːkəm'pəuz] vt. 使分解，使分裂，使腐烂
deformation [ˌdiːfɔː'meiʃən] n. 变形，形变，畸变
demonstrate ['demənstreit] vt. 表示，表明，示范，证实，证明，举例说明
deviator ['diːvieitə] n. 偏(离)；vi. 脱离，偏离；vt. 使违背，使脱离
dilatation [ˌdailei'teiʃən] n. 膨胀，扩张
distortion [dis'tɔːʃən] n. 扭曲，变形
equilibrium [ˌiːkwi'libriəm] n. 平衡
equivalence [i'kwivələns] n. 等价，同等
equivalent [i'kwivələnt] adj. 相当的，等价的；n. 等价物，相等物
formulation [ˌfɔːmju'leiʃən] n. 公式化，列方程式
hydrostatic [ˌhaidrəu'stætik] adj. (静)水压力的
invariant [in'vɛəriənt] adj. 不变的；n. 不变量
isotropic [aisəu'trɔpik] adj. 各向同性的
linear ['liniə] adj. 线性的
matrix ['meitriks] n. 矩阵；基体
mean [miːn, min] n. 平均数，中间，中庸；adj. 平均的 vt. 意谓，想要
normal ['nɔːməl] n. 正规，常态，法线；adj. 正常的，正规的，标准的，法向的
principle ['prinsəpl] n. 原理，法则，原则
proportionality [prəˌpɔːʃə'næliti] n. 比例，比例(性)，均衡(性)
separate ['sepəreit] vt. 使分离，分开；adj. 分开的，独立的；vi. 分开，隔离，分散
symmetry ['simitri] n. 对称

tensor ['tensə] $n.$ 张量
traction ['trækʃən] $n.$ 面力,应力,拖拉,牵引(力)
volume ['vɔljuːm] $n.$ 体积,容量

Lesson 13

Stress Concentrations

1. A problem frequently encountered is that of determining the stresses in the vicinity of a notch or similar irregularity in the shape of a body. The irregularities in the body, such as holes, cracks, or notches, always induce an elastic stress near the irregularity which may be considerably greater than the nominal stress calculated from the loads and the net cross sectional area of the body. In this case these local irregularities are of greatest interest.

2. One example of this stress-concentrating effect of an irregularity is the effect of a small hole in a very large plate which

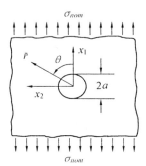

Fig.1 Stress concentration at a hole with a stress-free boundary in an infinite plate subjected to a uniaxial stress

is subjected to uniaxial tension (see Fig. 1). Since the surface of the hole must be stress free, the stress in the vicinity of the hole must be modified from the uniaxial tension. The introduction of the stress-free hole does not change the resultant forces on the plate, so that the effect of the hole should decrease with increasing distance from the hole. The solution to this problem is one of the many elastic solutions which are well known and may be found in many books on elasticity. In cylindrical coordinates, the stress acting in a tangential direction at the edge of the hole is given by

$$\sigma_{\theta\theta} = \sigma_{nom}(1 - 2\cos 2\theta), \quad \sigma_{\theta\theta} = \begin{cases} -\sigma_{nom} & \text{for } \theta = 0, \pi \\ 3\sigma_{nom} & \text{for } \theta = \pm \pi/2 \end{cases}$$

where σ_{nom} is the nominal stress when the hole is absent.

3. The maximum stress with the hole present is therefore three times the nominal stress or, stated another way, the hole has a stress concentration factor of 3 in a uniaxial state of stress. This solution for the effect of a hole in uniaxial tension in plane stress is very useful, since by adding two of these solutions directed along the two principal stress directions, one can determine the stress concentration factor for a hole in any plane-stress condition, provided that other boundaries of the body are sufficiently far from the hole.

4. The above solution indicates that local perturbations such as holes tend to raise the stress locally. However, the specialized case of a circular hole cannot be directly extended to other types of holes and notches. The case of the elliptical hole adds further insight into the nature of stress concentrations.

5. Consider a sheet in plane stress with an elliptical hole oriented so that the axes of the ellipse are parallel and

perpendicular to the tension direction (see Fig. 2). The stress concentration factor for this case is

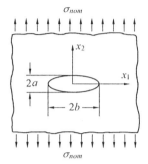

Fig. 2 Stress concentration at an elliptic hole with a stress-free boundary in an infinite plate subjected to uniaxial stress

$$\frac{\sigma_{max}}{\sigma_{nom}} = 1 + 2\frac{b}{a} \tag{1}$$

and the maximum stress is σ_{22} at the ends of the ellipse, $x_1 = \pm b$. Note that if $b > a$ the elliptic hole has a greater stress concentration factor than a circular hole, but if $b < a$ the stress concentration is less than for a circular hole.

6. The solution for an elliptic hole can be used to obtain approximate stress concentration factors for other shapes of holes. For this purpose, expression (1) can be changed so that the stress concentration factor is expressed as a function of the radius of curvature ρ at the end of the ellipse and the width of the hole perpendicular to the stress axis, $2b$. The value of ρ can be obtained by $\rho = a^2/b$. Substituting this expression for a in Eq. (1) gives the desired formula for the stress concentration factor:

$$\frac{\sigma_{max}}{\sigma_{nom}} = 1 + 2\sqrt{\frac{b}{\rho}} \tag{2}$$

7. St. Venant's principle indicates that the stress

concentration factor should be a strong function of the local radius of curvature at the point of maximum stress, but it should be much less sensitive to the shape of the boundary at large distances from this point. For this reason, the elliptic hole formula can be used to get approximate values of the stress concentration factor for other shapes of holes by approximating the latter with an elliptic hole having the same radius of curvature at the ends and the same overall length. By the use of this procedure, solutions for stress concentrations in a number of complicated geometries and states of loading have been obtained. For example, internal slots and holes of arbitrary shape can be modeled by ellipses with the same minimum radius of curvature and overall length, and external notches can be modeled by hyperbolas with the same minimum radius of curvature.

New Words and Expressions

approximate [ə'prɔksimeit] *adj.* 近似的; *vt.* 接近; *vi.* 接近于
arbitrary ['ɑːbitrəri] *adj.* 任意的
area ['ɛəriə] *n.* 区域,面积
circular ['səːkjulə] *adj.* 圆形的,循环的
concentration [ˌkɔnsen'treiʃən] *n.* 集中,浓缩,浓度,专心
coordinate [kəu'ɔːdinit] *n.* 坐标
crack [kræk] *n.* 裂缝
cross [krɔs] *n.* 十字,交叉,十字架; *adj.* 交叉的,相反的
　　　　 v. 使交叉,横过,勾画,错过,杂交
curvature ['kəːvətʃə] *n.* 曲率
cylindrical [si'lindrik(ə)l] *adj.* 圆筒的,柱状的
effect [i'fekt] *n.* 效果,影响,作用; *vt.* 引起,招致
elasticity [ilæs'tisiti] *n.* 弹性

ellipse [i'lips] *n*. 椭圆

elliptical [i'liptikəl] *adj*. 椭圆的

encounter [in'kauntə] *vt*. 遇见,相遇,碰见

factor ['fæktə] *n*. 因素,系数

formula ['fɔːmjulə] *n*. 公式

frequent ['friːkwənt] *adj*. 频繁的,时常发生的

function ['fʌŋkʃən] *n*. 函数,功能

hole [həul] *n*. 孔,洞

hyperbola [hai'pəːbələ] *n*. 双曲线

induce [in'djuːs] *vt*. 招致,导致,引起,感应

insight ['insait] *n*. 察看,洞察力

irregularity [iˌregju'læriti] *n*. 不规则,无规律,不规则(物)

local ['ləukəl] *adj*. 局部的,地方性的

modify ['mɔdifai] *vt*. 更改,修改,修正; *v*. 修改

net [net] *n*. 网; *adj*. 净的

nominal ['nɔminl] *adj*. 名义上的

notch [nɔtʃ] *n*. 缺口,凹槽,刻痕

orient ['ɔːriənt] *adj*. 东方的; *n*. 东方; *vt*. 定向,取向,为定…方位;使朝东

overall ['əuvərɔːl] *adj*. 全部的,全体的

parallel ['pærəlel] *n*. 平行; *adj*. 平行的

perpendicular [ˌpəːpən'dikjulə] *adj*. 垂直的,正交的; *n*. 垂线

perturb [pə'təːb] *vt*. 扰乱,使混乱

perturbation [ˌpəːtəː'beiʃən] *n*. 扰动,扰乱,摄动

principal ['prinsəp(ə)l, -sip-] *adj*. 主要的; *n*. 首长

principle ['prinsəpl] *n*. 原理

procedure [prə'siːdʒə] *n*. 程序,过程

radius ['reidjəs] *n*. 半径

raise [reiz] *n*. 上升,举起; *vt*. 提高,提出,升起,唤起

sectional ['sekʃənəl] *adj*. 截面的,部分的
sensitive ['sensitiv] *adj*. 敏感的,灵敏的
slot [slɔt] *n*. 狭槽,缝,细长孔
substitute ['sʌbstitjuːt] *n*. 代用品,代替者,替代品; *v*. 代替,替换,替代
tangential [tæn'dʒenʃ(ə)l] *adj*. 切线的
tension ['tenʃən] *n*. 张力,拉伸
uniaxial ['juːni'æksiəl] *adj*. 单轴的
vicinity [vi'siniti] *n*. 附近,邻近

Lesson 14

Buckling of Columns

1. The selection of the columns is often a very crucial part of the design of a structure because the failure of a column usually has catastrophic effects. Furthermore, columns are more difficult to design than bars in bending or torsion because their behavior is more complicated. If a column which is long compared to its width is subjected to axial force P, it may fail by buckling, that is, the deflection increases rapidly as the load P approaches a certain critical value. This value is known as the critical load P_{cri}. The buckling phenomenon is associated with the transition of the column configuration from a stable equilibrium condition to an unstable equilibrium condition when the critical load P_{cri} is reached.

2. In order to investigate the behavior of columns, we will begin by considering a slender, perfectly straight column of length L which is fixed at the lower end and free at the upper end [see Fig. 1(a)]. If the axial load P is less than the critical value, the bar remains straight and undergoes only axial compression. This straight form of equilibrium is stable, which means that if a lateral force is applied and a small deflection is produced, the deflection will disappear, and the bar will return to its straight form, when the lateral force is removed.

3. However, as P is gradually increased, a condition of neutral equilibrium is reached when P becomes equal to P_{cri}. At this load the column theoretically may have any small value of deflection, and a small lateral force will produce a deflection which does not disappear when the lateral force is removed. At higher values of the load the column is unstable and will collapse.

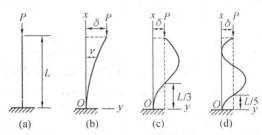

Fig. 1 (a) a slender column before buckling
(b) buckled mode shape for $n = 1$
(c) mode shape for $n = 3$
(d) mode shape for $n = 5$

4. The critical load for a column can be calculated by using the equation of the deflection curve. For the column shown in Fig. 1(b), the equation is

$$EIv'' = P(\delta - v) \qquad (1)$$

where δ is the deflection at the free end. Using the notation $k^2 = P/EI$, we can write the general solution of Eq.(1) in the form

$$v = C_1 \sin kx + C_2 \cos kx + \delta \qquad (2)$$

The boundary conditions at the built-in end of the column, $v = v' = 0$ gives $C_1 = 0$ and $C_2 = -\delta$, and the deflection curve becomes $v = \delta(1 - \cos kx)$. Using the boundary condition at the upper end of the column, $v = \delta$, we find

$$\delta \cos kL = 0 \qquad (3)$$

from which we conclude that either $\delta = 0$ or cos $kL = 0$.

5. If $\delta = 0$, there is no deflection of the column and hence no buckling. Such an event is represented in Fig. 1(a). The other possibility is that cos $kL = 0$, we see from Eq.(3) that δ can have any small value. The condition cos $kL = 0$ requires that $kL = n\pi/2$ where $n = 1, 3, 5, \cdots$. Thus, we can obtain an infinite number of critical loads

$$P_{cri} = \frac{n^2\pi^2 EI}{4L^2} \quad (4)$$

This equation shows that, as n is increased, the deflection curve has more and more waves in it. When $n = 1$, the curve has one-half of a wave, as shown in Fig. 1(b). The deflection curves for $n = 3$ and $n = 5$ are shown in Fig. 1(c) and (d) respectively. Although they represent theoretically possible modes of buckling for the column, they are of no practical interest because the column will buckle in the first mode which corresponds to the smallest critical load of the column.

6. Critical buckling loads for columns with simply supported ends and with fixed ends can be obtained from the solution of the preceding case. For example, it is evident from symmetry that the deflection curve of a column with hinged ends in the first mode of buckling will have a vertical tangent at the midpoint. Hence, each half of the column is in the same condition as the bar in Fig. 1(b), and the critical load is obtained from Eq. (4) ($n = 1$) by substituting $L/2$ for L, i.e., $P_{cri} = \pi^2 EI/L^2$. If the column is fixed at both ends, the deflection curve for the first buckling mode is a cosine curve having inflection points at distance $L/4$ from the ends. Therefore, the critical load is obtained by substituting $L/4$ for L, i.e., $P_{cri} = 4\pi^2 EI/L$.

7. From Eq. (4) we see that the critical load for a column is directly proportional to the flexural rigidity EI and inversely proportional to the square of the length. Thus, the critical load can be increased by increasing the moment of inertia I of its cross section. This result can be accomplished by distributing the material as far as possible from the centroid of the cross section. Hence, tubular members are more economical for columns than are solid members having the same cross-sectional area.

8. By diminishing the wall thickness of such sections and increasing the transverse dimension, the stability of the column is increased because I is greater. There is a lower limit for the wall thickness, however, below which the wall itself becomes unstable. Then, instead of buckling of the column as a whole, there will be localized buckling of the wall in the form of corrugations of wrinkling of the wall. This type of buckling is called local buckling and requires a more detailed investigation.

New Words and Expressions

buckle ['bʌkl] n. 屈曲,皱曲; v. 弄弯,皱曲,翘曲
built-in ['bilt'in] adj. 固定的,嵌入的
catastrophic [ˌkætə'strɔfik] adj. 灾难的
centroid ['sentrɔid] n. 质心
collapse [kə'læps] n. 倒塌,崩溃,失败; vi. 倒塌,崩溃,瓦解,失败
column ['kɔləm] n. 圆柱,列
compression [kəm'preʃ(ə)n] n. 压缩
corrugation [ˌkɔru'geiʃən] n. 起皱,波纹
crucial ['kruːʃiəl, 'kruːʃəl] adj. 决定性的,严厉的
deflection [di'flekʃən] n. 挠曲,偏向
diminish [di'miniʃ] v. (使)减少,(使)变小

distribute [dis'tribju(:)t] vt. 分布，散布
equation [i'kweiʃən] n. 等式，方程
equilibrium [ˌi:kwi'libriəm] n. 平衡
failure ['feiljə] n. 破坏，失败
flexural ['flekʃərəl] adj. 弯曲的，挠性的
hinge [hindʒ] n. 铰链，枢纽；v. 以…而定；以…为转移
inertia [i'nə:ʃjə] n. 惯性，惰性
infinite ['infinit] n. 无限；adj. 无穷的
inflection [in'flekʃən] n. 弯曲，屈曲
inverse ['in'və:s] n. 反面，倒数；adj. 相反的，逆向的，倒转的，反转的；v. 倒转
inversely adv. 相反地，倒转地
lateral ['lætərəl] adj. 侧面的，横向的
moment ['məumənt] adj. 片刻的，瞬间的，力矩的；n. 瞬间，矩，力矩
notation [nəu'teiʃən] n. 记号，注释
phenomenon [fi'nɔminən] n. 现象
proportional [prə'pɔ:ʃnl] adj. 比例的，成比例的，相称的
remove [ri'mu:v] vt. 移动，除去，移交；vi. 迁移，搬家
rigidity [ri'dʒiditi] n. 刚性，刚度
slender ['slendə] adj. 细长的，苗条的
symmetry ['simitri] n. 对称
tangent ['tændʒənt] adj. 切线的，相切的；n. 切线，[数]正切
torsion ['tɔ:ʃən] n. 扭转
transition [træn'ziʒən, -'siʃən] n. 转变，转换，跃迁
tubular ['tju:bjulə] adj. 管状的
vertical ['və:tikəl] adj. 垂直的，直立的
wave [weiv] n. 波动，波浪
wrinkle ['riŋkl] n. 皱纹，皱褶；v. 起皱

Lesson 15

What Are Dynamic Problems?

1. When a structure is subjected to dynamic loading, the whole or part of it is accelerated with the result that inertia forces are introduced. Due to the influence of inertia forces, the stresses vary during and after loading so that a particular state of stress exists only at a corresponding instant during the process. In many cases, however, when the loads are gradually applied or change slowly, the dynamic effect is insignificant and can be neglected. With suddenly applied loads the effect of inertia forces must be taken into account and in extreme cases such as impact or resonance vibration, the dynamic effect predominates.

2. As mentioned previously, the dynamic effect, i. e., the influence of inertia forces on the process of stress development in a body, depends on the dynamic loading conditions. Three groups of typical phenomena can be distinguished. These are (1) quasi-static states of stress, (2) vibrations, and (3) stress waves. The limits between these groups are not clearly defined, however, and frequently the phenomena associated with more than one group can occur in the same dynamic event.

3. The dynamic response of a body depends not only on the magnitude of the forces acting but also, to a decisive extent, on their rate of change. Thus, while stress waves are produced by the

change of forces, the frequency of these waves is determined by their rate of change. If the change of forces is due to the impact of a striking body, this means that the response of the body struck depends on the time of contact between the two bodies.

4. When the forces acting on a body change slowly so that the frequency is very low, the length of the wave is usually great compared with the dimensions of the body. In such extreme cases, the stress distribution is independent of the rate of the forces. Although the stresses vary in magnitude during the process, their distribution remains the same throughout and is identical with that under corresponding static loading. The external forces acting on the body are in equilibrium throughout the event and all stresses vanish when these forces cease to act. Problems in which the behavior follows this pattern are called quasi-static.

5. When the frequency of the loading cycle is of the same order as the resonance frequency of the body, the stress waves and their reflections cause vibrations, e. g., longitudinal or flexural vibrations. Due to inertia forces the stress distribution will differ to some extent from that in comparable static or quasi-static cases and the external forces are not in equilibrium throughout the event.

6. If the rate of change of the forces acting on a body corresponds with a high frequency, i. e., with the generation of waves which are short compared with the dimensions of the body, the effect of stress waves predominates. In such cases the stress distribution differs greatly from that produced under static or quasi-static conditions.

7. A problem frequently encountered is that of determining the

stress concentration factor under dynamic conditions involving stress waves or vibrations at a notch or other irregularity in the shape of a body. In such cases the procedure to be adopted depends on the relative dimensions of the wavelength and the notch. If the dimensions of the notch are small compared with the wavelength, the stress distribution in the neighborhood of the notch will be similar to that under comparable static loading. Such loading applied to a model of the relevant small part of the body will therefore produce the same stress distribution.

8. When the length of a stress wave is of the same order or smaller than the dimensions of a body or, for instance, of a notch in it, dynamic methods must be applied. This is also true in the case of vibrations. Since the stress concentration factor depends on the length of the stress wave involved, it is obvious that there is no generally applicable dynamic factor of stress concentration.

New Words and Expressions

accelerate [æk'seləreit] v. 加速,促进
cease [si:s] v. 停止,终了
concentration [ˌkɔnsen'treiʃən] n. 集中,集合,浓缩,专心
distinguish [dis'tiŋgwiʃ] v. 区别,辨别
distribution [ˌdistri'bju:ʃən] n. 分布,分配
dynamic [dai'næmik] adj. 动力的,动力学的,动态的
extreme [iks'tri:m] n. 极端; adj. 极端的,极度的
factor ['fæktə] n. 因数,系数
flexural ['flekʃərəl] adj. 弯曲的,挠曲的
frequency ['fri:kwənsi] n. 频率
identical [ai'dentikəl] adj. 同一的,相同的
impact ['impækt] n. 冲击; v. 撞击

inertia [i'nə:ʃjə] n. 惯性,惰性
irregularity [iˌregju'læriti] n. 不规则,无规律
longitudinal [lɔndʒi'tju:dinl] adj. 纵向的,经度的
neighborhood ['neibəhud] n. 附近,邻近
notch [nɔtʃ] n. 缺口,凹槽,刻痕
predominate [pri'dɔmineit] v. 主导,控制,成为主流
quasi-static adj. 准静态的
reflection [ri'flekʃən] n. 反射,反映
resonance ['rezənəns] n. 谐振,共振
response [ris'pɔns] n. 反应,响应
strike [straik] n. 罢工,打击; v. 撞击,冲击;罢工;
struck [strʌk] 'strike' 的过去式和过去分词
subject ['sʌbdʒikt] vt. 使受到,使服从; n. 科目,主题,主语
vanish ['væniʃ] vi. 消失,成为零
vibrate [vai'breit] v. 振动
vibration [vai'breiʃən] n. 振动
wave [weiv] n. 波,波浪,致意; vi. 波动,飘动,摇动,致意
wavelength ['weivleŋθ] n. 波长

Lesson 16

General Description of Waves

1. Waves appear to be disturbances in some sort of medium. In the case of the clothes line the 'medium' is the cord itself and the 'disturbance' is a displacement of part of the cord. In a similar way, the surface of a pool of water is capable of carrying a disturbance along. Here the 'medium' is the water and the 'disturbance' is an upward or downward movement of the surface. Sound waves in air fit into much the same mode. The 'medium' is the air itself and the 'disturbance' is a displacement of a region of the air. In general, the essential nature of a wave is a disturbance of some sort in a medium which, owing to the properties of the matter, changes either in form or position, or both, as time goes on.

2. Let us consider the 'medium' a little further. Although it enables a disturbance to be propagated, it itself does not move bodily along. For example the disturbance at one end of the clothes line is propagated along its length, but none of the particles of which the cord is composed actually moves from one end of the line to the other. So a wave is a means of transmitting energy from one point to another without any net transfer of matter. Moreover, it is a means of transmitting information from one point to another. It may be noticed that the light waves and

other forms of radiation such as X-rays, ultraviolet rays, infrared rays, and radio waves appear to require no medium whatsoever for their propagation. Indeed, they can travel through a vacuum, but we also describe them in the same way as other waves.

3. Waves in strings may be either transverse or longitudinal. For a transverse wave, the direction of travel is at right angles to the disturbance. Let us imagine that a string is stretched horizontally, and that one end is agitated with an up-and-down movement, then we would have a transverse wave with disturbance in the up-and-down direction moving along the length of the string. On the other hand, a longitudinal wave can be set up by taking one end of the string and successively stretching and releasing it along its own length. In this type of wave, the disturbance is in the direction of propagation. In fact, transverse and longitudinal waves have many properties in common with each other.

4. Solid rods are capable of sustaining three different types of wave. The first and simplest is the longitudinal wave which is propagated because of the tensile elastic properties of the rod. It is quite easy to excite such waves. If a rod of length about one meter is held firmly at its center and stroked along its length by a resined cloth, a longitudinal wave is propagated back and forth along the rod. It cannot be visually observed, but the effect of the wave can easily be audibly observed as a high-pitched sound of considerable purity. Because the rod is of comparatively small length, the reflection of the waves back along the rod when they reach either end becomes very important and determines the pitch of the note heard. Transverse waves may exist in rods, but are more difficult to produce. Finally, torsional waves may exist. If a rod is twisted

at one end, then the restoring torque causes a wave to be propagated. Here, the 'disturbance' is not a linear displacement, but an angular twist.

5. A membrane, for example the stretched skin on a drum, is the two-dimensional equivalent of a stretched string. Here, as in the string when any part of the skin is pushed in a direction perpendicular to its plane and then released, transverse waves are set up. These waves, unlike those on the string, spread out from the point of the initial disturbance in a way very similar to that in which surface waves on water spread out from a point of disturbance. The simplest type of two-dimensional wave is a 'straight-line' wave i.e., its direction of propagation is constant over the whole surface and its profile is the same along any line drawn in that direction.

6. Point sources of waves propagating into a three-dimensional medium produce spherical waves radiating outwards from the source at the center. This means that a detector placed at successively greater distances from the source records successively weaker responses since the total energy is being spread over the surface of a sphere of increasing surface area. This limits the range over which the detector can operate. In the case of sound waves, the point source can be represented by a loudspeaker, and the detector by a microphone or the ear. To increase the range it is possible to 'guide' the wave through a tube so that the energy can be concentrated to a definite direction. The speaking tube is an obvious example which is technically known as a waveguide.

New Words and Expressions

agitate ['ædʒiteit] v. 搅动, 摇动, 激动, 激励

audibly [ˈɔːdib(ə)li] *adv*. 可听见地
cord [kɔːd] *n*. 绳索，束缚
detector [diˈtektə] *n*. 发现者，侦察器，探测器，检波器
disturbance [disˈtɔːbəns] *n*. 打扰，干扰，扰动
drum [drʌm] *n*. 鼓，鼓声
excite [ikˈsait] *vt*. 刺激，激励，使兴奋，使激动
horizontal [ˌhɔriˈzɔntl] *adj*. 水平的，地平线的
infrared [ˈinfrəˈred] *adj*. 红外线的；*n*. 红外线
longitudinal [lɔndʒiˈtjuːdinl] *adj*. 纵向的，经度的
loudspeaker [ˈlaudˈspiːkə] *n*. 扩音器，喇叭
matter [ˈmætə] *n*. 物质，事件，问题，实质；*vi*. 有关系，要紧
medium [ˈmiːdjəm] *n*. 媒体，媒介，介质，中间物，方法，手段；*adj*. 中间的，中等的
membrane [ˈmembrein] *n*. 膜，隔膜
microphone [ˈmaikrəfəun] *n*. 扩音器，麦克风
mold [məuld] *n*. 模子，模具，铸模；类型，模型，形状，样板
note [nəut] *n*. 笔记，注解，注释，票据，纸币，音符；*vt*. 注意，记录，笔记
particle [ˈpɑːtikl] *n*. 粒子，点，质点，微粒
pitch [pitʃ] *n*. 音调，程度，强度，节距，间距，斜度，倾斜，树脂，沥青；*vt*. 投，掷，定位于
profile [ˈprəufail] *n*. 剖面，侧面，外形，轮廓
propagate [ˈprɔpəgeit] *v*. 传播，宣传，繁殖
radiate [ˈreidieit] *vt*. 放射，辐射，传播，广播；*vi*. 发光，辐射
radiation [ˌreidiˈeiʃən] *n*. 发散，辐射，放射，发光，发热
ray [rei] *n*. 光线，闪烁；*vi*. 射出光线；*vt*. 放射，显出
reflection [riˈflekʃən] *n*. 反射，反映，映象
region [ˈriːdʒən] *n*. 区域，地方，地区，(艺术，科学等的)领域
resin [ˈrezin] *n*. 树脂；*vt*. 涂树脂于

response [ris'pɔns] n. 回答，响应，反应
restore [ris'tɔ:] vt. 恢复，使回复
skin [skin] n. 皮，皮肤，外壳
spherical ['sferikəl] adj. 球的，球形的
stretch [stretʃ] v. 伸展，伸长；n. 一段时间，一段路程，伸展
string [striŋ] n. 线，细绳，一串
stroke [strəuk] n. 击，敲，(网球等)一击，(划船等)一划
successive [sək'sesiv] adj. 继承的，连续的
torque [tɔ:k] n. 扭矩，转矩
torsional ['tɔ:ʃənəl] adj. 扭力的，扭转的
transmit [trænz'mit] vt. 传输，传导，发射；vi. 发射信号，发报
transverse ['trænzvə:s] adj. 横向的，横断的
twist [twist] n. 一扭，扭曲 vt. 拧，绞，捻 vi. 扭曲，扭动
ultraviolet [ʌltrə'vaiələt] adj. 紫外的，紫外线的
vacuum ['vækjuəm] n. 真空，空间；adj. 真空的，产生真空的
visually ['vizjuəli] adv. 在视觉上地，真实地
wave [weiv] n. 波，波浪；vi. 波动，飘动，摇动
waveguide ['weivgaid] n. [电子]波导

Lesson 17

Potential Energy Method

1. The concept of potential energy is extremely important in structural mechanics. In the following discussion we will describe how potential energy is used in structural analysis and how it relates to strain energy and the displacement method. In addition, it will be shown that the potential energy can often be used for making approximate analyses of structures in cases where an exact analysis is not feasible.

2. The potential energy of any mechanical or structural system in some actual configuration is defined as the work, which will be done by all of the acting forces if the system is moved from that actual configuration to some reference configuration. In general, the reference configuration is often taken as the shape of the unloaded structure. Thus, the potential energy is the work done by all the acting forces when the structure is moved from its loaded configuration to its position when unloaded.

3. The acting forces for the structure consist of both external loads and internal forces. The internal forces may be taken as stresses for the problems of continual solids or stress resultants in the case of a beam, truss, or frame. The potential energy of the internal forces is clearly the strain energy U stored in the loaded structure, because if the structure is displaced from its actual to

its unloaded shape, the amount of work recovered is equal to the strain energy.

4. The potential energy of the external forces is negative, because each load on the structure does negative work if it is "backed up" from its final position to its initial position. Thus, the potential energy of the loads is

$$-\sum_{i=1}^{n} P_i \delta_i \tag{1}$$

where P_i represents a load on the structure, δ_i is the corresponding displacement, and n is the number of loads.

5. It should be noted especially that the potential energy of a load P_i is not the same as the work done by P_i during the loading of the structure. During the loading process, the force P_i gradually increases in magnitude from zero to its final value and the work done by this load is given by.

$$W = \int_0^{\delta_1} P \mathrm{d}\delta \tag{2}$$

The potential energy, on the other hand, is the work done by the force (acting at its final value) when it is moved from its final position back to the reference state.

6. For the purpose of analyzing a structure by the potential energy method, the unknow displacements $\delta_1, \delta_2, \cdots, \delta_n$ must be identified first. Then the strain energy U can be expressed as a function of those displacements. Also, it is assumed that all of the loads on the structure, denoted $P_1, P_2, \cdots, P_n$, correspond to the unknown displacements. Under these conditions, the total potential energy of a structural system is obtained by combining the strain energy of the structure and the potential energy of the loads, so that

$$\Pi = U - \sum_{i=1}^{n} P_i \delta_i \qquad (3)$$

This expression for the total potential energy applies for any elastic structure, whether it behaves linearly or nonlinearly.

7. By taking the partial derivative of the potential energy with respect to any one of the unknown displacements δ_i, the following equation can be obtained

$$\frac{\partial \Pi}{\partial \delta_i} = \frac{\partial U}{\partial \delta_i} - P_i \qquad (4)$$

From Castigliano's first theorem we know that $P_i = \partial U / \partial \delta_i$, and therefore, the n simultaneous equations are derived and expressed as follows

$$\frac{\partial \Pi}{\partial \delta_1} = 0 \quad \frac{\partial \Pi}{\partial \delta_2} = 0 \quad \cdots \quad \frac{\partial \Pi}{\partial \delta_n} = 0 \qquad (5)$$

8. From the conceptual point of view, Eqs. (5) have special significance because they show that the equilibrum conditions of the structure are satisfied when the potential energy of the structure has a stationary value, which may be a minimum, maximum, or neutral value. Thus, Eqs. (5) may be considered as the equations of equilibrium for the displacement method. Alternatively, Eqs. (5) can be taken as a mathematical representation of the principle of stationary potential energy.

9. The principle of stationary potential energy states that if the potential energy of an elastic structure (linear or nonlinear) is expressed as a function of the unknown displacements, then the structure will be in equilibrium when the displacements have such values as to make the total potential energy assume a stationary value. Usually the structure is in stable equilibrium, and then the total potential energy is a minimum. Under these conditions, Eqs.

(5) represent the principle of minimum potential energy. For unstable structures, the potential energy may have either a maximum value or a neutral value.

10. The application of the principle of stationary potential energy leads to as many simultaneous equations as there are unknown displacements. These equations are the equilibrium equations of the displacement method, and they can be solved for the unknown displacements. If the structure behaves linearly, Eqs.(5) yield the equilibrium equations of the stiffness method, which may be considered as a special case of the displacement method. However, it must be realized that the principle of stationary potential energy is a basic principle in applied mechanics and is used in practice for a great variety of complex structures. In addition, it can also be used in many ways other than in structural analysis.

New Words and Expressions

addition [ə'diʃən] n. 加,加法
complex ['kɔmpleks] adj. 复杂的,合成的,多元的,综合的
concept ['kɔnsept] n. 概念
conceptual [kən'septʃuəl, -tjuəl] adj. 概念上的
configuration [kənˌfigju'reiʃən] n. 构造,结构 外形
denote [di'nəut] vt. 指示,表示,(符号)代表
derivative [di'rivətiv] n. 导数,微商;派生的事物; adj. 引出的
energy ['enədʒi] n. [物]能量
exact [ig'zækt] adj. 精确的,准确的,原样的
expression [iks'preʃən] n. 表达,表达式,符号
feasible ['fi:zəbl] adj. 可行的
frame [freim] n. 框架;构架,骨架结构

in addition *adv.* 另外
negative ['negətiv] *adj.* 负的；阴性的；消极的
neutral ['nju:trəl] *adj.* 中性的；*n.* 中性；中立国
partial ['pɑ:ʃəl] *adj.* 部分的，局部的，偏的，偏微分的
potential [pə'tenʃ(ə)l:] *adj.* 潜在的；*n.* 潜能，潜力
recover [ri'kʌvə] *vi.* 痊愈，回复；*vt.* 重新获得
resultant [ri'zʌltənt] *n.* 组合，合量；*adj.* 组合的，合成的
simultaneous [ˌsiməl'teinjəs] *adj.* 同时的，同时发生的
solid ['sɔlid] *n.* 固体
stationary ['steiʃ(ə)nəri] *adj.* 稳定的，定常的，驻[定]的，稳态的，固定的
stiffness ['stifnis] *n.* 坚硬，刚性，刚度
truss [trʌs] *n.* 一束，构架
unload ['ʌn'ləud] *vi.* 卸货，卸载；*vt.* 摆脱
yield [ji:ld] *n.* 屈服 *v.* 产出 *vi.* (~ to) 屈服于

Lesson 18

Principle of Virtual Work

1. The concepts of virtual displacements and virtual work are usually introduced during the study of statics, where they are used to solve problems of static equilibrium. The word "virtual" implies that the quantities are purely hypothetical and that they do not exist in a real or physical sense. Thus, a virtual displacement is an imaginary displacement that is arbitrarily imposed upon a structural system. It is not an actual displacement, such as a deflection caused by loads acting on a beam. The work done by the real forces during a virtual displacement is called virtual work.

2. The principle of virtual displacements is applicable to a rigid body that is held in equilibrium by the action of a set of loads, which may include forces, couples, and distributed loads. The rigid body may be given a virtual displacement consisting of a translation in any direction, a rotation about any axis, or a combination of rotation and translation. In all instances the virtual work done by the forces will be zero if the body is in equilibrium. Usually we must restrict the virtual displacement to a very small displacement in order that the lines of action of the forces will not be altered during the virtual displacement.

3. For use in structural analysis, we must extend the principle of virtual displacements to include the case of a deformable

structure. For a structure of this kind, we must take into account not only the virtual work of the external forces but also the virtual work associated with the internal forces. In order to show how this is accomplished, let us consider a structure which is assumed to be loaded in a completely general fashion by forces, bending couples, torques, and distributed loads. The structure is, of course, at rest and in equilibrium under the action of the various loads.

4. Assume now that the structure is given a virtual deformation consisting of a small change in its deformed shape. This virtual deformation is imposed upon the structure in some unspecified manner and is completely independent of the fact that the structure has already been subjected to real deformation caused by the loads acting on it. Such real deformation has definite magnitude dictated by the nature of both the loads and the structure. The virtual deformation, however, represents an additional deformation that is imparted to the structure, which previously was in an equilibrium configuration under the action of the real loads.

5. The only restriction on the virtual deformation is that it must represent a deformed shape that could actually occur physically. In other words, the virtual change in shape must be compatible with the conditions of support for the structure and must maintain continuity between elements of the structure. Except for that restriction, the virtual change in shape may be arbitrarily imposed on the structure. It should not be confused with the deformed shape of the structure caused by the real loads.

6. During the virtual deformation each element of the structure will be displaced to a new location and also will be deformed in

shape. Therefore, the forces acting on an element will perform virtual work. Let us denote the total amount of this virtual work by dW_e. This work, which is associated with one element, may be considered as composed of two parts: (1) the work dW_r due to the displacement of the element as a rigid body and (2) the work dW_d associated with the deformation of the element. Thus.

$$dW_e = dW_r + dW_d \qquad (1)$$

7. Because the element is in equilibrium, the virtual work dW_r done by the forces during the displacement of the element as a rigid body must be zero, and hence the preceding equation reduces to

$$dW_e = dW_d \qquad (2)$$

This equation states that the total virtual work done by all forces acting on the element during its virtual displacement is equal to the virtual work done by those same forces during only the virtual deformation of the element. If we now sum up the virtual work terms in Eq.(2) for all elements of the structure, we get

$$\int dW_e = \int dW_d \qquad (3)$$

where it is understood that the integrations are performed over the entire structure.

8. The integrals in Eq. (3) can be given a simple interpretation. The integral on the left-hand side of the equation is the total virtual work done during the virtual deformation of the structure by all the forces, both loads and stresses, acting on all faces of all elements. We may note, however, that the sides of each element are in direct contact with the sides of adjacent elements. Therefore, the virtual work of the stresses acting on one element will exactly cancel the virtual work of the equal and

opposite stresses acting on adjacent elements. The only remaining virtual work is the work of the external forces acting on the external boundaries of the elements. Thus, we reach the conclusion that the integral on the left-hand side of Eq. (3) is equal to the virtual work of the external forces acting on the structure. We will refer to this quantity as the external work and designate it by W_{ext}.

9. The term on the right-hand side of Eq. (3) was obtained by integrating the virtual work associated with the deformation of an element. This work includes the effects of all forces acting on the element, both stresses and external loads. However, when an element deforms, only the stresses perform any work. Thus, the second term in Eq. (3) actually represents the virtual work of the stresses alone. This virtual work is equal to the work done by the stresses when the elements on which they act are deformed virtually. The total amount of this virtual work, obtained by summing for all elements, is called the internal work and is denoted by W_{int}. Thus, Eq. (3) becomes

$$W_{ext} = W_{int} \qquad (4)$$

10. Eq. (4) represents the principle of virtual work, and it may be stated as follows: If a deformable structure in equilibrium under the action of a system of loads is given a small virtual deformation, then the virtual work done by the external loads is equal to the virtual work done by the internal forces (or stresses). It should be noted that the properties of the material of the structure are not taken into consideration in the development of the principle of virtual work. Therefore, the principle of virtual work applies to all structures irrespective of whether the material behaves linearly or nonlinearly, elastically or inelastically.

New Words and Expressions

adjacent [ə'dʒeisənt] adj. 邻近的,接近的
alter ['ɔ:ltə] v. 改变
arbitrarily ['ɑ:bitrəri] adv. 任意地,专横地,随便地
axis ['æksis] n. 轴
boundary ['baundəri] n. 边界,分界线
compatible [kəm'pætəbl] adj. 谐调的,相容的,一致的,兼容的
configuration [kən,figju'reiʃən] n. 结构,构造,外形
continuity [,kɔnti'nju(:)iti] n. 连续性,连贯性
couple ['kʌpl] n. (一)对,(一)双,配偶,力偶,力矩; vt. 连接,结合; vi. 结合,结婚
deflection [di'flekʃən] n. 偏斜,偏转,挠曲,挠度
deformable [,di'fɔ:məbl] adj. 可变形的
designate ['dezigneit] vt. 指明,指出; v. 指定,指派
dictate [dik'teit] v. 支配,决定,指示,口述,口授
equilibrium [,i:kwi'libriəm] n. 平衡
hypothetical [,haipəu'θetikəl] adj. 假设的,假定的
impart [im'pɑ:t] vt. 给予,分给,传授,告知,透露
impose [im'pəuz] vt. 强加,把…强加给,征税; vi. 利用,施影响
linear ['liniə] adj. 线的,直线的,线性的
restrict [ris'trikt] vt. 限制,约束,限定
restriction [ris'trikʃən] n. 限制,约束
rigid ['ridʒid] adj. 刚硬的,刚性的,严格的
rotating [rəu'teiʃən] n. 旋转
torque [tɔ:k] n. 扭矩,转矩
translation [træns'leiʃən] n. 翻译,译文;转化,转换;[物][数]平移
virtual ['və:tjuəl,-tʃuəl] adj. 虚的,实质的,[物]有效的,事实上的
work [wə:k] n. 工作;[物]功,作品; v. (使)工作,(使)运转

Lesson 19

Introduction to Computer Hardware

1. The modern digital computer can be defined as an ' electronic device for high speed automatic information processing'. This powerful computational device can receive the information provided by the user, operate upon it, and produce new information. For a better understanding of this process of acquisition, processing, and delivering of information, we should identify the basic components of a computer, and analyze their functions. These components are shown in Fig. 1 in a schematic manner.

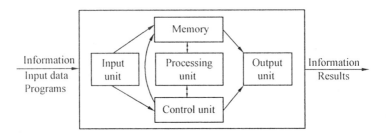

Fig. 1 Basic components of a computer

2. The information supplied by the user is received by the input unit or reader. The user does not give that information in a completely arbitrary manner, but will have to follow some specific

rules, to allow for its interpretation. The physical media used to register information is known as information support. Examples of common information support are punched cards, punched paper tapes, magnetic disks, etc.. For each type of information support there is a type of input unit which can assimilate it.

3. The user supplies the computer with information which is composed of data and instructions. The set of instructions given to the computer, defining the operations required to achieve the solution is known as a program or computer program. Program and data are not, in general, read simultaneously or intermixed. The program is normally read first. Then the computer operates according to the instructions included in the program which indicates to the computer when and how to read the data. This process is normally called execution or processing of the program.

4. The information which enters the computer is immediately transferred to the computer memory. A computer can have several memories, including a primary memory, which will always exist, and one or more secondary memories, which may or may not exist. The function of a memory is to store information for short or long periods of time. The primary memory can be considered as the 'heart' of the computer, since all the information that it receives, or generates, must pass through the primary memory.

5. The primary memory can be conceived as a large collection of small 'cells' which are normally called memory positions. Each memory position is identified by a number, called memory address. The information read or generated by the computer is subdivided into information units, called words. A word is further subdivided into characters. The number of characters in a word defines the word length. The content of a memory position is a

word, which can be put into or taken from the memory position through its address. Most primary memories are magnetic core devices.

6. The extremely high utilization of the primary memory does not permit large amounts of information to be stored in it for long periods of time, especially if the information is not required for current processing. In this case, much cheaper secondary memories are used with a capacity many times greater than that of the primary memory.

7. When the amount of information to be handled is too large for the primary memory, it is stored in the secondary memory devices and the parts of that information required for the processing, are transferred to the primary memory, as necessary. The information is transferred back to the secondary memories when no longer required. Secondary memory devices can be fixed or removable magnetic disks, magnetic tapes, magnetic drums, etc.. It is interesting to note that in a small volume, corresponding to one magnetic tape or disk, several millions of characters can be stored.

8. The processing of the information stored in the primary memory is carried out by the processing unit. This unit has the capacity to perform arithmetic operations, and to take logical decisions. It receives information from the primary memory, subdivided in words, operates upon that information, and places the new information generated in the primary memory.

9. The computer delivers to the user the results of a solution through the output unit. Again an information support will be used. The information supports for output can be continuous sheets of paper obtained from the printer, magnetic tapes,

punched cards, microfilm, paper with drawings obtained from a plotter, etc.. It is also possible to have an output unit consisting of a screen where results can be displayed, for instance, in the form of diagrams. Sometimes, these devices can produce a 'hard copy' of that information if required. In general, a computer will have more than one output unit, one or more of which will be printers.

10. In general, a computer can perform several simple tasks. It can receive and store information, perform elementary arithmetic operations, take simple logical decisions, and deliver information. All the operations which are carried out inside a computer are controlled by its control unit. This unit is the brain of the computer, in the sense that it initiates, supervises, and directs the activities of the remaining units. Since the computer can perform large quantities of complex computations in an automatic way, it is also called an 'electronic brain'.

New Words and Expressions

acquisition [ˌækwi'ziʃən] n. 获得,获得物;采集,收集 [pl.]学识,技能
arithmetic [ə'riθmətik] n. 算术,算法; adj. 算术学的
assimilate [ə'simileit] v. 吸收,使同化
cell [sel] n. 单元; 细胞; 电池
conceive [kən'siːv] vt. 构思,认为
core [kɔː] n. 核心,果心 v. 成核
deliver [di'livə] vt. 递送,交付
digital ['didʒitl] adj. 数字的
drum [drʌm] n. 鼓; 磁鼓; 卷筒
execute ['eksikjuːt] vt. 执行,实行; 处死
hardware ['haːdwɛə] n.硬件,五金器具

identify [ai'dentifai] *vt*. 使等同于,认为一致(with);认出,识别,鉴别; *vi*.(成为)一致(with)
input ['input] *n*. 输入 *v*. 输入
instruction [in'strʌkʃən] *n*. 指令;教导
interpretation [in͵tə:pri'teiʃən] *n*. 解释,说明;诠释,描述;翻译,译码
logical ['lɔdʒikəl] *adj*.(合乎)逻辑的; 合理的
memory ['meməri] *n*. 记忆,内存;存储(器)
plotter ['plɔtə] *n*. 绘图仪;策划者
process [prə'ses] *n*. 程序,进行; *vt*. 加工,对…处置
punch [pʌntʃ] *vt*. 冲压,开洞; *n*. 打洞器,冲压机
register ['redʒistə] *n*. 寄存器;注册,记录,登记簿; *vt*. 记录,登记,把…挂号; *vi*. 登记,注册,挂号
remain [ri'mein] *vi*. 保持,保留,剩余
schematic [ski'mætik] *adj*. 图解的,示意的 *n*. 图表
screen [skri:n] *n*. 屏,银幕;掩蔽物; *vt*. 掩蔽,放映,拍摄
simultaneous [͵siməl'teinjəs] *adj*. 同时的
supervise ['sju:pəvaiz] *v*. 监督,管理,指导

Lesson 20

Introduction to Computer Software

1. A computer can perform an operation according to proper instructions. The set of all the instructions which a computer accepts constitutes the machine language, or absolute language of that computer. The machine language instructions are always expressed by numeric codes. Each instruction normally consists of one operation code, and one or more parameters or arguments. For instance, the sequence

    60099098100

    65100097101

can represent two instructions written according to a given machine language.

2. Let us assume that the operation code 60 (first two digits of the first instruction) indicates addition. Then the first instruction could be a request to add the content of the memory position of address 099 (first argument), with the content of the memory position of address 098 (second argument), placing the result in the memory position of address 100 (third argument).

3. The second instruction has an operation code 65. Let us assume that it is used to request a multiplication. In that case, the second instruction might mean that the contents of the memory positions of addresses 100 and 097 are to be multiplied, placing the

result in the memory position of address 101.

4. This hypothetical example attempts to illustrate how a machine language program is written. The difficulties implicit are evident. Each instruction refers to one or more memory positions, designated by their numeric addresses, which requires careful planning of the memory utilization, before writing the program. In this type of programming, errors are frequently made, it is obviously very hard to detect and correct them. On the other hand, machine languages are not the same for different computers.

5. To solve some of these problems, symbolic languages were introduced. In these languages symbolic names are used for the operation codes. The memory positions are also referred to by symbolic names, which is called symbolic addressing. For instance, in a hypothetical symbolic language the two previous machine language instructions could be written as

  ADD A,B,C

  MUL C,D,E

Where the first instruction would indicate addition (code ADD) of the contents of the memory positions A and B, placing the results in the memory position C. Similarly, the second instruction would indicate multiplication (code MUL) of the contents of the memory positions C and D, placing the results in the memory position E.

6. Clearly, the symbolic language is much simpler than machine language. However, a computer cannot directly accept this type of language, since it only 'understands' its machine language. It is then necessary to translate the symbolic language program to a machine language program before it can be processed. This translation can be done directly by the computer,

in an automatic way, using a special translation program, which is normally called an assembler. The assembler, residing in the computer memory, is a program which receives a symbolic language program as data, and produces as a result an equivalent machine language program which can be processed by the computer. The symbolic languages are sometimes called assembler languages.

7. To solve practical engineering problems, the symbolic language is still very hard to apply. Thus, more powerful languages, which are called algorithmic languages, are developed and currently used in the world. Algorithmic languages enable the solution of a problem to be defined as a sequence of algebraic formulae, including some logical conditions and miscellaneous instructions. For instance, in a hypothetical algorithmic language the previous instructions will be written as

$$E = D * (A + B)$$

Which is called a statement. This type of programming is highly efficient since it allows a convenient notation to be used, similar to that of algebra.

8. It is obvious that a computer will not accept such languages directly, but require translation to machine language. This translation is also done automatically by the use of a special program called a compiler. In this case, each statement can be translated into many machine instructions, by a translation process called compilation. Among the algorithmic languages, the best known is FORTRAN, which is almost universally available. Other algorithmic languages are ALGOL, BASIC, PASCAL and COBOL etc..

New Words and Expressions

algorithm ['ælgəriðəm] n. 算法；演段；编码
algorithmic adj. 算法的
argument ['ɑːgjumənt] n. 自变量，变元
assembler [ə'semblə] n. 汇编语言，汇编程序
code [kəud] n. 代码，代号，密码，编码 vt. 把……编码
compilation [ˌkɔmpi'leiʃən] n. 编辑；编译
compile [kəm'pail] vt. 编译
compiler [kəm'pailə] n. 编辑者，[计] 编译器
constitute ['kɔnstitjuːt] vt. 构成，组成
designate ['dezigneit] vt. 指定，指明
equivalent [i'kwivələnt] adj. 相当的 n. 等价物
error ['erə] n. 误差；错误，过失
formula ['fɔːmjulə] n. 公式
hypothesis [hai'pɔθisis] n. 假设
implicit [im'plisit] adj. 暗示的，含蓄的
logical ['lɔdʒikəl] adj. 合乎逻辑的，合理的
miscellaneous [misi'leinjəs, -niəs] adj. 各种的，杂的
multiply ['mʌltipli] v. 乘；繁殖
notation [nəu'teiʃən] n. 记号，注释
numeric [njuː'merik] adj. 数值的，数字的
parameter [pə'ræmitə] n. 参数，参量
reside [ri'zaid] vi. 住，居留
software ['sɔftwɛə] n. 软件
statement ['steitmənt] n. 指令，陈述
symbolic [sim'bɔlik] adj. 符号的，象征的

Lesson 21

Metallic Materials

1. It is unimaginable for a mechanical engineer to seriously ignore the realm of engineering materials, regardless of his particular field of interest. One of the first things a new engineer learns in his profession is that lack of proper engineering materials and lack of knowledge of those that are available can impose sharp limitations on engineering design. Therefore, it is necessary to provide mechanical engineers with a basic knowledge of the mechanical behavior of common structural materials. However, it has been one of the most difficult subjects to learn because of its diverse nature and its heavy dependence on empiricism. Our modern understanding of the theory of material science is as yet incomplete.

2. Modern industry needs considerable quantities of metals, one of the most important of these is iron. However, iron has little use in its pure state, but when combined with other substances into various alloys, it becomes the widely used engineering material. Metals consisting of iron combined with some other substances are called ferrous metals, such as steel. Steel which contains very little carbon will be milder than steel which contains a higher percentage of carbon, up to the limit of about 1.5%. A certain number of non-ferrous metals, including aluminium and

copper, are also important, but even today the majority of our engineering products are of iron or steel. Here, a few typical metals are described as follows:

3.(1) **Steel**: Steel is an alloy based on iron and small amount of carbon, usually less than 1%. Various other alloying elements are often added to steel for specific end uses. It is the most commonly used engineering material due to its high modulus as well as its low cost. The modulus is one of the most important parameters in structural applications. Other attractive features of steel are high strength and ease of processing. There are many grades of steel for various applications. They are classified by their chemical composition.

4. Commercially available steels and their uses may be divided into the following groups:

a) Plain carbon steel is the cheapest type of steel. It is primarily used for structural purposes. It is available in commercial form as bars, plates, channels, etc.

b) High-strength steels are low-alloy steels which are used in structures where the strength requirement cannot be met by plain carbon steel.

c) Alloy steels have better harden ability than plain carbon steels. They are generally used for machine parts but rarely for structural purposes because of the increased cost.

d) Ultrahigh-strength steels are alloy steels with exceptionally high strength. These steels are used in applications requiring high strengths, such as aircraft landing gear, turbine shafts, etc.

e) Stainless steels are high-alloy steels which have more than 12% chromium content. Stainless steel is used where corrosion is a problem.

f) Tool steels are high-alloy steels with tungsten or molybdenum as the main alloying elements. They are used for molds, dies and cutting tools.

5. (2) **Aluminium**: After steel, aluminium is the most commonly used metal. It is available in many forms, and is much easier to machine and form than steel. Its advantages are light weight, good thermal conductivity, high corrosion resistance in air and water, and high reflectivity.

6. (3) **Magnesium**: Magnesium is the lightest structural material, its density being only 2/3 that of aluminium. Magnesium alloys have high strength-to-weight ratios. It is used to make office machines and luggage.

7. (4) **Copper**: Copper is mainly used where its high electrical and thermal conductivities are useful, as in electrical transmission lines and refrigerators.

8. (5) **Brass**: Brass is an alloy of copper and zinc. It is easily machined, formed, and soldered, and has better corrosion resistance than copper and steel. It is used to make bearings, valves, plumbing fittings, and shell casings.

New Words and Expressions

alloy ['ælɔi] $n.$ 合金
aluminium [ˌælju:'minjəm] $n.$ 铝
bar [bɑ:(r)] $n.$ 条,棒;酒吧
bearing ['bɛəriŋ] $n.$ 轴承;忍受
carbon ['kɑ:bən] $n.$ 碳
casing ['keisiŋ] $n.$ 箱,包装,套管
channel ['tʃænl] $n.$ 通道,渠道,管路

chromium ['krəumjəm] *n*. 铬
composition [kɔmpə'ziʃən] *n*. 组成,成分
corrosion [kə'rəuʒən] *n*. 腐蚀
density ['densiti] *n*. 密度
die [dai] *n*. 冲模 *v*. 死亡
diverse [dai'və:s] *adj*. 不同的,变化多的
empiricism [em'pirisizəm] *n*. 经验论,经验主义
ferrous ['ferəs] *adj*. 铁的,含铁的
gear [giə] *n*. 齿轮
impose [im'pəuz] *vt*. 把…强加于
limitation [ˌlimi'teiʃən] *n*. 限制,局限性
magnesium [mæg'ni:zjəm] *n*. 镁
metallic [mi'tælik] *adj*. 金属的
mild [maild] *adj*. 温和的,软性的
mold [məuld] *n*. 模子,模型; *v*. 铸造,模压
molybdenum [mə'libdinəm] *n*. 钼
parameter [pə'ræmitə] *n*. 参数,参量
plain-carbon steel 碳素钢
plumb [plʌm] *n*. 铅锤,铅弹; *adj*. 垂直的; *vt*. 使垂直,探测; *vi*. 垂直
realm [relm] *n*. 领域,王国
reflectivity [ˌri:flek'tiviti] *n*. 反射率
shaft [ʃɑ:ft] *n*. 轴
shell [ʃel] *n*. 壳,壳体
solder ['sɔldə,'sɔ(:)-] *n*. 焊接剂; *v*. 焊接
stainless ['steinlis] *adj*. 不锈的
substance ['sʌbstəns] *n*. 物质,本质
transmission [trænz'miʃən] *n*. 传输,播送,发射,传动
tungsten ['tʌŋstən] *n*. 钨
turbine ['tə:bin,-bain] *n*. 涡轮机

valve [vælv] *n*. 阀,阀门
zinc [ziŋk] *n*. 锌

Lesson 22

Nonmetallic Materials

1. Although metallic materials are widely used in industrial applications, nonmetallic materials, such as plastics, ceramics, concrete and wood, are also very important in our life. In contrast, nonmetallic materials have many characteristics, due to their inherent nature, that are quite different from those of more conventional metallic materials. Here, some of the commonly used nonmetallic materials are depicted below.

2. **Plastics**

   Thermoplastics, which are usually processed by raising their temperature to either the melting point or the glass transition temperature, are usually molded or extruded. Thermosetting plastics, which do not soften with increase in temperature, are usually molded from their liquid components either under pressure or in open molds. Plastics have been becoming more important engineering materials during the past two decades. The main reasons are that the price of plastics has been decreasing with the increase in consumption rate and that the physical properties of various plastics have improved to meet engineering requirements.

3. Some typical plastics are described as follows:

   (1) **Polyethylene**:

   Polyethylene is one of the most commonly used plastics due

to its many desirable properties. It is lighter than water, translucent, highly pliable, non-toxic, odorless, tough, quite stable chemically, and easy to process. It is used to make bottles, thin films for laundry bags, toys, chemical containers, electrical insulation, pipes, and linings in corrosive applications. It is one of the cheapest plastics.

(2) **Polyvinyl chloride (PVC)**:

Another commonly used low-cost plastics is PVC, Since it is self-extinguishing, it is used in applications where fire resistance is important. It is used to make tiles, house siding, pipes, photograph records, shoes, and garments.

(3) **Polyamide (nylon)**:

Nylon is one of the well-known synthetic plastics. Nylon possesses outstanding resistance to impact and fatigue, low coefficient of friction, excellent abrasion resistance, chemical stability, and good dielectric properties. It is self-extinguishing and can be processed by conventional means. It is used to make gears, cams, fibers for brush bristles and fabrics, machine parts, tubing, appliance parts, rope and fishing lines.

(4) **Epoxy Resins**:

Epoxy is one of the best known thermosetting plastics due to its good physical properties such as good bonding characteristics, high temperature stability, high dielectric strength, high resistivity, good chemical resistance, and reasonably good mechanical properties. Mechanical properties of epoxy resins can be improved a great deal by the addition of fillers such as glass or cloth fibers.

4. **Ceramics**

A ceramic is defined as a combination of one or more

metals with a nonmetallic element, usually oxygen. Most of the ceramics are brittle but have high melting points and high hardness. Ceramics are widely used to make high-temperature containers such as crucibles, bricks, heat shields, semiconductors, various insulators, abrasives, and pigments. Glass is a ceramic, belonging to the general class of amorphous silicon oxides with very high viscosity. It is very brittle, and does not conduct heat or electricity well. It is relatively cheap due to the abundance of its raw materials. Glass is used for containers, windows, optical devices, insulators, and in the form of fibers for reinforcing materials and fabrics.

5. Ceramic parts are normally manufactured from micropowder. Ceramic powders are either processed cold or hot into final shapes. Cold-pressed powders must be sintered in a kiln for agglomeration. During pressing, binders such as liquid wax are sometimes added to obtain 'green' strength. Ceramic powders are also processed by first wetting them with liquid (usually water) and then casting the slurry into a mold or by extruding it through a die. The final step of the process involves firing the molded piece in a kiln.

6. **Cements and Concrete**

Concrete is an aggregate of sand, gravel, and cement which bonds together when the cement undergoes hydration. Concrete is one of the major structural materials used in construction of buildings, roads, dams and other large fixed structures.

7. **Wood**

Wood is one of the oldest and most commonly used engineering composite materials in the construction of houses and other simple structures. Its main advantages are ease of processing, relatively good overall physical properties, and low cost.

New Words and Expressions

abrasion [ə'breiʒən] n. 磨擦,磨损
abrasive [ə'breisiv] n. 研磨料
agglomeration [əˌglɔmə'reiʃən] n. 聚结,结块
aggregate ['ægrigeit] n. 聚集体
amorphous [ə'mɔːfəs] adj. 非晶体的,无定形的,无组织的
binder ['baində] n. 用以绑缚之物, 粘合剂, 胶, 胶合物
bond [bɔnd] n. 结合(物),粘结(剂),粘合,联结,合同; v. 结合
brittle ['britl] adj. 脆性的
cam [kæm] n. 凸轮
cement [si'ment] n. 水泥
ceramic [si'ræmik] adj. 陶瓷的, 陶器的; n. 陶瓷制品
chloride ['klɔːraid] n. 氯化物
concrete ['kɔnkriːt] n. 混凝土; adj. 具体的,有形的
corrosive [kə'rəusiv] adj. 腐蚀性的
crucible ['kruːsibl] n. 坩锅
depict [di'pikt] vt. 描述, 描写
die [dai] n. 冲模 v. 死亡, 熄灭
dielectric [ˌdaii'lektrik] n. 电介质 adj. 非传导性的,绝缘的
epoxy [e'pɔksi] adj. 环氧的
extinguish [iks'tiŋgwiʃ] vt. 熄灭,根除,取消使消失;使暗淡;压制
extrude [eks'truːd] vt. 挤出, 压出, 挤压成
fatigue [fə'tiːg] n. 疲劳
fiber ['faibə] n. 纤维
filler ['filə] n. 装填物

gear [giə] n. 齿轮
gravel ['grævəl] n. 砂砾,碎石
hydration [hai'dreiʃən] n. 水合,水合作用
impact ['impækt] n. 冲击,撞击,碰撞,冲突; vt. 撞击
inherent [in'hiərənt] adj. 固有的,内在的
insulation [,insju'leiʃən] n. 绝缘,隔离
kiln [kiln, kil] n. 窑,炉,干燥炉
lining ['lainiŋ] n. 衬里,内层
melt [melt] n. 熔化 v.(使)熔化
mold [məuld] n. 模子,模型; v. 铸造,模压
nonmetallic ['nɔnmi'tælik] adj. 非金属的
nylon ['nailən] n. 尼龙
odor ['əudə] n. 气味
oxide ['ɔksaid] n. 氧化物
oxygen ['ɔksidʒən] n. 氧
pigment ['pigmənt] n. 颜料,色素
plastic ['plæstik, plɑ:stik] n. 塑胶,塑料制品; adj. 塑胶的;塑性的
pliable ['plaiəbl] adj. 易弯的,柔顺的
polyamide [pɔli'æmaid] n. 聚酰胺,尼龙
polyethylene [,pɔli'eθili:n] n. 聚乙烯
polyvinyl [,pɔli'vainil] adj. 聚乙烯基的
polyvinyl chloride n. 聚氯乙烯
reinforce [,ri:in'fɔ:s] vt. 加强,加固
resin ['rezin] n. 树脂
resistivity [,ri:zis'tiviti] n. 抵抗力,电阻系数
shield [ʃi:ld] n. 屏蔽,防护物,护罩,盾,盾状物; vt.(from) 保护,防护; v. 遮蔽
silicon ['silikən] n. 硅

sinter ['sintə] vt. 烧结
slurry ['slə:ri] n. 泥浆
synthetic [sin'θetik] adj. 合成的,人造的
thermoplastic [ˌθə:məu'plæstik] adj. 热塑性的; n. 热塑塑料
thermosetting [ˌθə:məu'setiŋ] adj. 热固的
tile [tail] n. 砖瓦,瓷砖,瓦片
toxic ['tɔksik] adj. 有毒的
translucent [trænz'lju:snt] adj. (半)透明的
viscosity [vis'kɔsiti] n. 粘性,粘质,粘滞性[度]
wax [wæks] n. 蜡

Lesson 23

Composite Materials

1. In general, a composite material is a material with several distinct phases combined in such a way as to increase its structural efficiency. This is due to the fact that several different materials can be combined to obtain the optimum physical and chemical properties. Normally, the composite consists of a reinforcing material, e.g., fiber or whisker, supported in a binder or matrix material. The reinforcing material is normally the load carrying medium in the material, and the matrix serves as a carrier, protector, and load splicing medium around the reinforcement. The current developments are pointed toward combinations of unusually strong, high modulus fibers and organic, ceramic, or metal matrices. Such materials promise to be far more efficient than the commonly-used structural materials.

2. Composite materials have a long history of usage. Their beginnings are unknown, but all recorded history contains references to some form of composite material. For example, straw was used by the Israelites to strengthen mud bricks. Plywood was used by the ancient Egyptians when they realized that wood could be rearranged to achieve superior strength and resistance to thermal expansion as well as to swelling owing to the presence of moisture. Medieval swords and armor were

constructed with layers of different materials. More recently, various advanced composites that have high strength-to-weight and stiffness-to-weight ratios have become important in weight-sensitive applications such as aircraft and space vehicles.

3. There are three commonly accepted types of composite materials:

(i) Fibrous composites which consist of fibers in a matrix,

(ii) Laminated composites which consist of layers of various materials,

(iii) Particulate composites which are composed of particles in a matrix.

4. Since numerous multiphase composites exhibit more than one characteristic of the classes, the classification scheme is arbitrary and imperfect. Nevertheless, the system should serve to acquaint the reader with the broad possibilities of composite materials. The basic types of composite materials are described as follows.

5. Fiber-reinforced composites such as boron-epoxy and graphite-epoxy consist of fibers in a matrix. The fibers, or filaments, are the principal reinforcing or load-carrying agent. They are typically strong and stiff. The matrix is to support and protect the fibers and to provide a means of distributing load among and transmitting load between the fibers. Naturally, fibers and whiskers are of little use unless they are bound together to take the form of a structural element which can take loads.

6. Long fibers in various forms are inherently much stiffer and stronger than the same material in bulk form. For example, ordinary plate glass fractures at stresses of only a few thousand pounds per square inch, yet glass fibers have strengths of 400 000

to 700 000 psi in commercially available forms. Obviously, the geometry of a fiber is somehow crucial to the evaluation of its strength.

7. More properly, the paradox of a fiber having different properties from the bulk form is due to the more perfect structure of a fiber. The crystals are aligned in the fiber along the fiber axis. Moreover, there are fewer internal defects in fibers than in bulk material. A whisker has essentially the same near crystal-sized diameter as a fiber, but generally is very short and stubby. Thus, a whisker is more perfect than a fiber and exhibits even higher properties.

8. A lamina is usually a single layer of flat material which consists of unidirectional fibers or woven fibers in a matrix. Since a laminate is composed of several such layers, the behavior of a single layer forms the basis or building block with which the properties of a laminate are described. The major purpose of lamination is to tailor the directional dependence of strength and stiffness of a material to match the loading environment of the structural element. Thus, lamination can be used to combine the best aspects of the constituent layers so as to achieve a more useful material. Examples of laminated fiber-reinforced composites include tennis rackets, missile cases, fiberglass boat hulls, aircraft wing panels and body sections, etc.

9. Particulate composites consist of particles of one or more materials in a matrix of another material. The particles can be either metallic or nonmetallic as can the matrix. The most common example of a nonmetallic particle system in a nonmetallic matrix, indeed the most common composite material, is concrete. Concrete is particles of sand and rock that are bound together by a

mixture of cement and water that has chemically reacted and hardened. Nonmetallic particles such as ceramics can be suspended in a metal matrix. The resulting composite is called a cermet. Two common classes of cermets in various industrial applications are oxide-based and carbide-balled composites.

10. Glass is a type of commonly used ceramic, belonging to the general class of amorphous silicon oxides with very high viscosity. It is very brittle, and does not conduct heat or electricity well. It is relatively cheap because of the abundance of its raw materials and due to ease of processing. There are many special grades of glass, such as Pyrex and Vycor, for various purposes. Pyrex is resistant to thermal shock, due to its low coefficient of thermal expansion, while Vycor is used as the material for vessels where diffusion of elements from the vessel is not desirable. Glass is also used for containers, windows, optical devices, insulators, and in the form of fibers for reinforcing materials and fabrics.

New Words and Expressions

acquaint [ə'kweint] vt. 使熟知，使认识
amorphous [ə'mɔːfəs] adj. 无定形的，无组织的
armor ['ɑːmə] n. 盔甲，装甲
boron ['bɔːrən] n. 硼
bulk [bʌlk] n. 大块，体积
carbide ['kɑːbaid] n. 碳化物
ceramic [si'ræmik] n. 陶瓷，陶器；adj. 陶器的
cermet ['səːmet] n. 金属陶瓷
composite ['kɔmpəzit, -zaitː] n. 复合材料；adj. 合成的
constituent [kən'stitjuənt] n. 成分，要素 adj. 构成的

crucial ['kru:ʃiəl,'kru:ʃəl] *adj.* 决定性的,严厉的
diffusion [di'fju:ʒən] *n.* 扩散,散播,蔓延
epoxy [e'pɔksi] *adj.* 环氧的
fiber ['faibə] *n.* 纤维
filament ['filəmənt] *n.* 单纤维,细丝
graphite ['græfait] *n.* 石墨
hull [hʌl] *n.* 壳,船体
laminate ['læmineit] *n.* 层合板
layer ['leiə] *n.* 层
matrix ['meitriks] *n.* 基体,基质;矩阵
mud [mʌd] *n.* 泥
organic [ɔ:'gænik] *adj.* 有机的;器官的,组织的
oxide ['ɔksaid] *n.* 氧化物
panel ['pænl] *n.* 嵌板,仪表板
paradox ['pærədɔks] *n.* 悖论,诡辩,自相矛盾的话
particulate [pə'tikjulit,-leit] *n.* 微粒,颗粒;*adj.* 微粒的
phase [feiz] *n.* 相,位相,阶段
plywood ['plaiwud] *n.* 夹板,层合板
reinforce [ˌri:in'fɔ:s] *vt.* 加强,加固,增援
silicon ['silikən] *n.* 硅
splice [splais] *vt.* 拼接,接合,粘连;*n.* 接合,拼接,结合
straw [strɔ:] *n.* 稻草,麦管
stubby ['stʌbi] *adj.* 粗而短的
swell [swel] *n.* 肿胀,膨胀;*v.* (使)膨胀,增大
viscosity [vis'kɔsiti] *n.* 粘稠,粘性
whisker ['hwiskə] *n.* 晶须,胡须

Lesson 24

Behavior of Composite Materials

1. A composite material is composed of two or more distinct materials which are combined together on a macroscopic scale to form an ideal material for structural applications. The advantage of composites is that they usually exhibit the best qualities of their constituents and often some qualities that neither constituent possesses. Therefore, composite materials have many characteristics that are different from more conventional engineering materials. Some characteristics are merely modifications of conventional behavior, others are totally new and require new analytical and experimental procedures.

2. Most common engineering materials are homogeneous and isotropic. The term homogeneous means uniform. That is, as one moves from point to point in the material, the material properties, i. e., stiffness, thermal coefficient of expansion, thermal conductivity, etc., remain constant. The material properties are not a function of position in the material. The term isotropic indicates that the material properties at a point in the body are not a function of orientation. In other words, the material properties remain constant regardless of the reference coordinate system at a point. Therefore, for an isotropic material, all planes which pass

through a point in the material are planes of material property symmetry.

3. In contrast, composite materials are often inhomogeneous, or heterogeneous and non-isotropic, or more generally anisotropic. An inhomogeneous body has non-uniform properties over the body, i.e., the properties are a function of position in the body. An anisotropic body has material properties that are different in all directions at a point in the body. There are no planes of material property symmetry. Again, the properties are a function of orientation at a point in the body.

4. It is known that the individual ply or lamina of a fibrous composite has three mutually perpendicular planes of symmetry for the material constants. The intersection of the three planes forms the axes of the coordinate system. Since the lamina has three perpendicular planes of symmetry, it can be considered to be an orthotropic material on the macroscopic level. Also, the lamina may be considered homogeneous on the macroscopic scale. The set of axes which are parallel and perpendicular to the fiber direction are termed the lamina principal axes. Obviously, an orthotropic body has three mutually perpendicular planes of material symmetry. Thus, the properties are a function of orientation at a point in the body.

5. The inherent anisotropy of composite materials leads to mechanical behavior characteristics that are quite different from those of conventional isotropic materials. For example, the isotropic, orthotropic, and anisotropic materials give different deformation modes under loading of normal stress and shear stress. For isotropic materials, normal stress causes extension in the direction of the applied stress and contraction in the

perpendicular direction. Also, shear stress causes only shearing deformation.

6. For orthotropic materials, like isotropic materials, normal stress in a principal material direction results in extension in the direction of the applied stress and contraction perpendicular to the stress. However, due to different properties in the two principal material directions, the contraction can be either more or less than the contraction of a similarly loaded isotropic material with the same elastic modulus in the direction of the load. Shear stress causes shearing deformation, but the magnitude of the deformation is independent of the various Young's moduli and the Poisson's ratios. That is, the shear modulus of an orthotropic material is, unlike isotropic materials, not dependent on other material properties.

7. For anisotropic materials, application of a normal stress leads not only to extension in the direction of the stress and contraction perpendicular to it, but to shearing deformation. Conversely, shearing stress causes extension and contraction in addition to the distortion of shearing deformation. This coupling between both loading modes and both deformation modes is also characteristic of orthotropic materials subjected to normal stress in a non-principal material direction.

8. The foregoing characteristics of composite materials can be observed and demonstrated by a simple test. Cloth is an orthotropic material composed of two sets of interwoven fibers at right angles to each other. If it is subjected to a stress at 45° to fiber direction both stretching and distortion occur.

New Words and Expressions

characteristic [ˌkærɪktəˈrɪstɪk] *adj*. 特有的,表示特性的,典型的; *n*. 特性,特征
coefficient [kəʊɪˈfɪʃənt] *n*. 系数
composite [ˈkɒmpəzɪt,-zaɪt:] *n*. 复合材料; *adj*. 合成的
conductivity [ˌkɒndʌkˈtɪvɪtɪ] *n*. 传导率
constituent [kənˈstɪtjuənt] *n*. 成分,要素; *adj*. 构成的
contraction [kənˈtrækʃən] *n*. 收缩,缩减
coordinate [kəʊˈɔːdɪnɪt] *n*. 坐标
coupling [ˈkʌplɪŋ] *n*. 耦合,联结; *adj*. 耦合的
deformation [diːfɔːˈmeɪʃən] *n*. 变形,形变,畸变
distortion [dɪsˈtɔːʃən] *n*. 扭曲;变形;失真
expansion [ɪksˈpænʃən] *n*. 膨胀
fibrous [ˈfaɪbrəs] *adj*. 纤维的
heterogeneous [ˌhetərəʊˈdʒiːnɪəs] *adj*. 异质的,非均匀的
homogeneous [ˌhɒməʊˈdʒiːnjəs] *adj*. 均匀的,同质的
intersection [ˌɪntə(ː)ˈsekʃən] *n*. 交叉,交集,相交;横断
isotropic [aɪsəʊˈtrɒpɪk] *adj*. 各向同性的
lamina [ˈlæmɪnə] *n*. 层板,薄层
mode [məʊd] *n*. 模态,状态,模式
modulus [ˈmɒdjʊləs] *n*. 模量,模数,系数
moduli [ˈmɒdjʊlaɪ] *n*. modulus 的复数
normal [ˈnɔːməl] *adj*. 正常的;垂直的,正交的;法向的;正态的;标准的; *n*. 法线;正交垂直线;常态;标准
orientation [ˌɔː(ː)rɪenˈteɪʃən] *n*. 方向,方位,取向
orthotropic [ˌɔːθəʊˈtrɒpɪk] *adj*. 正交各向异性的
ply [plaɪ] *n*. 层板; *v*. 铺层
principal [ˈprɪnsəp(ə)l,-sɪp-] *adj*. 主要的; *n*. 首长,主犯

stiffness ['stifnis] *n*. 刚度,坚硬
symmetry ['simitri] *n*. 对称
thermal ['θə:məl] *adj*. 热的

Lesson 25

Basic Deformations of Materials

1. When a body is subjected to loads, either from forces acting on its external surface or from the influence of gravity or similar "forces" which act throughout the body, stresses and deformation are produced within the body. The study of the effect of forces on continuous bodies forms the subject of continuum mechanics. An essential part of the formulation of problems in continuum mechanics is a description of the relationship between the stresses acting on an element of the body and the deformations which occur in that element.

2. Here, deformation is taken to mean the change in the geometric shape of a body. Depending on the nature of the engineering materials and the magnitude of the applied force, the materials can deform in many different ways. It can deform elastically, plastically, viscoelastically, or in a viscous manner. Each of these deformations may be briefly defined and characterized as follows:

3. *Elastic Deformation*

Elastic deformation may be defined as a reversible deformation, i.e., after the applied load is removed, the body returns to its original shape and all stored energy can be recovered. Any time a load is applied, there is a corresponding elastic deformation regardless of whether the stresses are shear, normal or hydrostatic. Therefore, if the magnitude of the applied load is given, the corresponding deformation can be determined uniquely.

4. The physical process involved is a simple stretching of atomic bonds by changing the distance between atoms. Nearly all crystalline materials at sufficiently low stresses behave elastically. Most metals at low stresses and ceramics are elastic. Partially crystalline polymers with no preferred orientation are also essentially elastic at low temperatures. The material properties which characterize the elastic nature of the isotropic material are Young's modulus E, shear modulus G, bulk modulus K, and Poisson's ratio υ. For isotropic materials only two of these properties are independent.

5. *Plastic Deformation*

Plastic deformation is a permanent deformation, i.e., after the applied load is removed, the body remains deformed and net work has been done. The physical process involves the sliding of atoms past each other, permanently changing their relative positions. In the applications normally encountered with metals, the normal stress does not significantly affect the sliding process. Therefore, it may be stated that only the shear stress can and does induce plastic deformation in metals.

6. The degree of deformation depends on the loading history and therefore cannot be uniquely specified in terms of stress. Some of the important parameters involved are the critical shear stress for plastic deformation, and work-hardening rate. For most quasi-static loading conditions, plastic deformation is time-independent, i.e., it does not depend on the duration of loading.

Most metals at high stresses exhibit plastic properties. At high temperatures, metals undergo a time-dependent type of plastic deformation called creep.

7. *Viscous Deformation*

Viscous deformation is a permanent deformation which is characterized by a time rate of deformation which is proportional to the applied load. Therefore, a viscous material can be deformed substantially by a small load if the duration of loading is long. Net work has to be done to deform viscous materials. The viscous deformation is normally induced by shear stresses only. However, the rate of deformation is influenced by the hydrostatic stress. This type of viscous behavior is exhibited by metals at high temperature and by plastics even at room temperature. Most fluids behave in a viscous manner. The viscous behavior of materials is characterized by specifying the viscosity.

8. *Viscoelastic Deformation*

Viscoelastic deformation occurs in certain materials such as plastics. It has aspects similar to both the elastic and viscous behavior. Therefore, the deformation of viscoelastic is partially recoverable, but is also time and rate dependent. The viscous work done during deformation is not recoverable. The elastic portion of deformation is induced by any stress components, whereas the viscous portion is governed by only the shear stresses. Viscoelastic materials are characterized by the relaxation modulus and viscosity.

New Words and Expressions

bond [bɔnd] *n*. 键;结合;债券,合同; *v*. 结合
ceramic [si'ræmik] *adj*. 陶瓷的,陶器的; *n*. 陶瓷,陶瓷制品

characterize ['kæriktəraiz] vt. 描绘…的特性,具有…特征;描绘,刻画
continuous [kən'tinjuəs] adj. 连续的,持续的
continuum [kən'tinjuəm] n. 连续体,连续介质
creep [kri:p] vi. 爬(动),蠕动;蠕变; n. 爬行,蠕动;蠕变
crystalline ['kristəlain] adj. 结晶性的,晶体的
deformation [ˌdi:fɔ:'meiʃən] n. 形变,变形,畸变
element ['elimənt] n. 元素,单元
gravity ['græviti] n. 地心引力,重力
hydrostatic [ˌhaidrəu'stætik] adj. 静水力学的,流体静力(学)的
induce [in'dju:s] vt. 引起,招致
isotropic [aisəu'trɔpik] adj. 各向同性的
net [net] adj. 净的,最终的;n. 网,网络,网状物
parameter [pə'ræmitə] n. 参数,参量
polymer ['pɔlimə] n. 聚合物
quasi-static ['kweisai-'stætik] adj. 准静态的,准静力的
reversible [ri'və:səbl] adj. 可逆的,可恢复的
slide [slaid] v. (使)滑动,(使)滑行; n. 滑;幻灯片
stretch [stretʃ] v. 伸展,延伸,伸长,张开
viscoelastic [ˌviskəui'læstik] adj. 粘弹性的
viscous ['viskəs] adj. 粘的,粘性的,粘滞的

Lesson 26

Failure Modes of Materials

1. After a certain amount of deformation, most materials eventually fracture, i. e., if the applied load is continuously increased, solids separate into two or more pieces unless the material is viscous. Under certain loading conditions some materials may rupture, where ultimate failure occurs when the cross-sectional area is reduced to zero. Fracture may be classified into different types on the basis of the behavior of the material prior to fracture and the loading conditions which cause the fracture.

2. **Brittle Fracture:** Brittle fracture occurs when the deformation which precedes fracture is predominantly elastic, i. e., there is little or no prior deformation. Glass and ceramics fracture in a brittle manner with essentially no preceding plastic deformation.

3. Many metals also fracture in a brittle manner under suitable conditions. However, in the case of metals, some plastic strain does occur in thin layers of the material at the fracture surface. Since the region which deforms plastically is of limited extent and forms only a small percentage of the volume of the body, the average strain and overall deflection of the body are still predominantly elastic and no appreciable permanent shape change

occurs before fracture.

4. Many glassy polymers also fracture in a brittle manner, but as in the case of metals, permanent deformation occurs near the fracture surface. Since the energy which must be supplied to propagate a brittle crack is usually less than the elastic strain energy released by the growth of the crack, brittle cracks can grow without additional work being done by the applied loads. For this reason, brittle cracks are often able to grow at very high velocities, comparable to the speed of sound in the material.

5. **Ductile Fracture**: Ductile fracture occurs when fracture is preceded by plastic deformation of a large percentage of the volume of the body. Ductile fracture differs from brittle fracture in that a certain amount of plastic deformation of the material is required to produce conditions favorable for fracture. Because of the plastic deformation required to produce the fracture, ductile fracture is preceded by considerable permanent change in the shape of the body. Therefore, the work which must be done by the external loads in order to produce fracture is much larger than the elastic energy stored in the body. Most structural metals fracture in a ductile manner at temperatures at or above room temperature.

6. **Fatigue Fracture**: When a body is subjected repeatedly to a load which is less than that required to cause fracture in a single application, it may fracture. This type of fracture is defined as fatigue fracture. As in the case of brittle fracture, fatigue fracture is often not preceded by general plastic deformation of the body. Fatigue fracture is in many ways similar to brittle fracture of metals except that the crack grows only a small amount on each cycle of loading. Metals which are exceedingly ductile under

monotonic loading will fracture by fatigue without ever undergoing any general plastic deformation.

7. **Creep Fracture**: Fracture in materials which are used at high temperatures where deformation occurs by creep is often called creep fracture. On a macroscopic basis, creep fracture is similar to ductile fracture in that it is preceded by general permanent deformation of the body. On a microscopic basis the processes which give rise to creep fracture are often different from those which occur at low temperatures.

8. The stress state which effects the fracture process is very complicated. It is known that plastic deformation occurs primarily in response to shear stress, fracture which involves pulling the atoms of a solid apart to create new surfaces occurs primarily in response to tensile stress. Because of this difference, the state of stress can have a great effect on whether a material deforms plastically or fractures.

9. For example, plastic deformation cannot occur under a state of hydrostatic tension because the shear stress is zero, but fracture can occur under this state of stress. Thus, a normally ductile material could presumably be made to fail in a brittle manner by subjecting it to a large hydrostatic tension.

10. Conversely, a normally brittle metal can be made to undergo large plastic strain if a hydrostatic compression is superimposed on a shear stress so as to make all of the principal stresses compressive.

New Words and Expressions

brittle ['britl] *adj.* 脆性的,脆弱的
ceramic [si'ræmik] *adj.* 陶瓷的,陶器的; *n.* 陶瓷,陶瓷制品

compression [kəm'preʃ(e)n] n. 压缩,浓缩,压榨
crack [kræk] n. 裂缝,破裂
creep [kri:p] vi. 爬(动),蠕动;蠕变; n. 爬行,蠕动;蠕变
cycle ['saikl] n. 周期,循环; [':] v. (使)循环,(使)轮转
deflection [di'flekʃən] n. 挠曲,挠度,歪斜
ductile ['dʌktail] adj. 韧性的,易延展的
exceeding [ik'si:diŋ] adj. 超越的,非常的
failure ['feiljə] n. 破坏,失败
fatigue [fə'ti:g] n. 疲劳
glassy ['glɑ:si] adj. 玻璃状的
hydrostatic [ˌhaidrəu'stætik] adj. 静水力学的,流体静力(学)的
layer ['leiə] n. 层
monotonic [mɔnəu'tɔnik] adj. 单调的
polymer ['pɔlimə] n. 聚合物
predominant [pri'dɔminənt] adj. 支配的,主要的,占主导地位的
presumably [pri'zju:məbəli] adv. 推测上,大概
primary ['praiməri] adj. 原始的,主要的
propagate ['prɔpəgeit] v. 传播,蔓延,繁殖;宣传
rupture ['rʌptʃə(r)] v. 断裂,破裂,裂开 n. 破裂,断裂
solid ['sɔlid] n. 固体; adj. 固体的,实心的,坚固的
superimpose ['sju:pərim'pəuz] vt. 重叠,叠加,添加
ultimate ['ʌltimit] adj. 最后的,最终的,根本的 n. 最终
velocity [vi'lɔsiti] n. 速度
viscous ['viskəs] adj. 粘性的,粘滞的,胶粘的

Lesson 27

Plastic Behavior of A Tensile Bar

1. To investigate the plastic behavior of materials, it is common to carry out an experiment by deforming a standard tensile specimen, and the constitutive relations can be plotted in terms of the engineering normal stress and the engineering normal strain. The engineering normal stress is defined as the current force acting on a unit original area perpendicular to the direction of the force. The engineering normal strain is defined as the change in the length divided by the original length.

2. The uni-axial stress-strain curve of metals such as aluminum, copper, and cold-worked steel is shown in Fig. 1. At the onset of loading, metals deform elastically until a critical strain

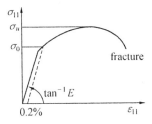

Fig. 1 Typical engineering stress-engineering strain curve of metals

or stress is reached, after which they deform p lastically. The critical stress which characterizes the transition from the elastic to plastic deformation is called the yield strength. As shown in Fig. 1, the yield strength is defined to be the stress at a plastic strain of 0.2%.

3. In the elastic region, Hook's law can describe the stress-strain relationship in terms of two elastic constants, such as Young's modulus E and Poisson's ratio υ. Similar relationships are needed to describe the constitutive relations of metals which are deforming plastically. However, the mathematical description of the stress-strain relations in the plastic region is complicated by the fact that the stress is not linearly dependent on the strain and that the constitutive relationship is a function of the prior deformation history.

4. In the plastic strain range, the flow stress depends on the entire plastic strain history and the plastic strain increment $d\varepsilon_{11}^p$ is related to an increment of stress through the local slope of the work-hardening curve $d\sigma_{11}/d\varepsilon_{11}^p$. Plastic stress-strain curves must be determined experimentally just as elastic constants must be.

5. When plastic deformation is very large, the change in the area of cross section and the change in the length of the element may be so large that the engineering normal stress and normal strain may not truly represent the state of loading and deformation. Therefore, it is sometimes more convenient to discuss the plastic state of deformation in terms of the true normal stresses and true normal strains. The true normal stress is defined as the normal force divided by the true cross-sectional area. The true normal strain is defined as the change in the length of the specimen over the current length.

6. For uniform deformation, the true normal strain becomes

$$\varepsilon_{11} = \sum_{i=0}^{i=t} \frac{\Delta l_i}{l_i} = \int_{l_0}^{l_t} \frac{\mathrm{d}l}{l} = \ln \frac{l_t}{l_0} \qquad (1)$$

where $l_i = l_1$, l_2, etc. are the lengths of the element at each incremental step of loading. Since the final expression is given in terms of a logarithmic function, the true strain is sometimes referred to as the logarithmic strain, or, occasionally, as the natural strain.

7. The stress-strain curve of Fig.1, replotted in terms of true stress and true strain, is shown in Fig.2. Note that in the true stress-true strain curves the stress continues to increase until fracture, instead of dropping off as it does in the engineering stress-strain curve. For operational simplicity, actual stress-strain curves are often idealized to fit simple mathematical relations.

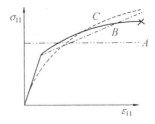

Fig.2 True stress-true strain curve obtained from Fig.1

8. One of the most commonly used idealizations is the rigid-perfectly plastic shown by the dotted line A in Fig.2. In this case, the effect of work hardening is disregarded by choosing a flow stress level such that the plastic work done is equal to the true plastic work done according to the real stress-strain curve. Another commonly employed idealization is the constant work hardening rate, which is shown by the bilinear stress-strain curve (curve B) in Fig.2. A more realistic stress-strain relationship is one of the power-law type (curve C), i.e.,

$$\sigma_{11} = \sigma_0(\varepsilon_{11})^n \qquad (2)$$

The exponent n indicates the work hardening rate, and the yield stress σ_0 corresponds to the flow stress at unit strain.

9. When a specimen is loaded to the plastic state, plastic deformation does not occur uniformly throughout the specimen. It begins at the smallest or the weakest cross section, one of which must exist since no specimen has a perfectly uniform cross section or is perfectly homogeneous. With plastic deformation this deforming section becomes smaller in diameter and work hardens. When the increase in the flow stress due to work hardening is greater than the increase in stress due to the localized decease in diameter, this section becomes stronger than other sections, and a new section deforms plastically. As long as this process continues, 'uniform' plastic deformation of the specimen occurs.

10. When the rate of work hardening cannot compensate for the localized increase in the applied stress due to the decrease in the cross-sectional area, deformation continues to occur in the same localized area. This is called necking. Plastic instability is controlled by the rate of work hardening and is important in many structural applications.

New Words and Expressions

bilinear [bai'liniə] *adj.* 双线性的

characterize ['kæriktəraiz] *vt.* 描绘…的特性,具有…特征; 描绘,刻画

compensate ['kɔmpənseit] *v.* 补偿;均衡,平衡;校正

constitutive ['kɔnstitju:tiv] *adj.* 构成的;要素的;本质的;本构的

critical ['kritikəl] *adj.* 临界的;批判的,评论性的

define [di'fain] *vt.* 定义

diameter [dai'æmitə] n. 直径
disregard [ˌdisri'gɑːd] vt. 不理,不顾,不管; n. 不理,不顾,忽视
dot [dɔt] n. 点,圆点
exponent [eks'pəunənt] n. 指数,幂阶,方次
flow [fləu] n. 流动,流程; vi. 流动,涌流,飘扬
fracture ['fræktʃə] n. 断裂,破裂; v. (使)破碎,(使)破裂
function ['fʌŋkʃən] n. 函数;功能,作用
harden ['hɑːdn] vt. 使变硬,使坚强; vi. 变硬,变冷酷
homogeneous [ˌhɔməu'dʒiːnjəs] adj. 均匀的,同质的
idealization [aiˌdi(ː)əlaiz] n. 理想化
increment ['inkrimənt] n. 增量,增加
incremental [inkri'mentəl] adj. 增量的,增加的
instability [ˌinstə'biliti] n. 失稳,不稳定
linear ['liniə] adj. 线性的
local ['ləukəl] adj. 局部的;地方的
logarithmic [ˌlɔgə'riθmik, -iðm-] adj. 对数的
necking ['nekiŋ] n. 颈缩
normal ['nɔːməl] adj. 正常的;垂直,正交的;法向的;正态的;
　　　　　标准的; n. 法线;正交垂直线;常态;标准
onset ['ɔnset] n. 开始,进攻
plastic ['plæstik, plɑːstik] n. 塑料; adj. 塑性的
plot [plɔt] n. 图,图表; vt. 绘…的图;标绘;划分
power ['pauə] n. 强度;乘方;功率;能力,力量
prior ['praiə] adj. 在先的
relation [ri'leiʃən] n. 关系,联系;亲戚
slope [sləup] n. 斜率,倾斜
specimen ['spesimin, -mən] n. 试件,样品
uni-axial adj. 单轴的
uniform ['juːnifɔːm] adj. 均匀的,统一的,一律的

yield [ji:ld] *v.* 屈服；产生 *n.* 产量，收益；屈服(点)

Lesson 28

Yield Criteria

1. The stress-strain relationships presented for tensile test are given in terms of the normal stress and normal strain. Such a representation is possible since only uniaxial loading is considered. However, in many applications of engineering materials the loading is multiaxial. The immediate question is then: "How can the constitutive relations for a material under multiaxial loading be determined and represented without plotting all of the stresses and all of the corresponding strains?"

2. An answer will be provided by an extension of the considerations for the uniaxial loading test. The uniaxial behavior of a material represented by the tensile stress-strain curve can be generalized to cases of multiaxial loading by making use of the following assumptions: *plastic deformation occurs in response to shear stress*; *and plastic deformation does not change the volume of a body*.

3. The concept that the behaviors in different cases are identical when the maximum shear stresses are identical could be used to develop constitutive relations for the more general state of loading. Unfortunately, this procedure does not lend itself to simple mathematical description. Therefore, it is more common to compare different states of stress and strain by using as parameters the equivalent (or effective) stress $\bar{\sigma}$ and the equivalent plastic

strain increment $d\bar{\varepsilon}^p$. It will be shown that these two parameters are closely related to the maximum shear stress and the maximum shear strain increment.

4. The equivalent stress $\bar{\sigma}$ may be written in terms of the second invariant of the deviator stresses J'_2, i.e.,

$$\bar{\sigma} = \sqrt{3}(J'_2)^{\frac{1}{2}} = \sqrt{\frac{3}{2}(\sigma'_{ij}\sigma'_{ij})^{\frac{1}{2}}} \qquad (1)$$

Since the equivalent stress $\bar{\sigma}$ is nearly proportional to the maximum shear stress, $\bar{\sigma}$ can be used in place of the uniaxial normal stress $\bar{\sigma}_{11}$ to characterize the nature of loading on a multiaxially loaded member.

5. The equivalent strain increment $d\bar{\varepsilon}$ may be defined as

$$d\bar{\varepsilon} = \sqrt{\frac{2}{3}[(d\varepsilon_{ij})(d\varepsilon_{ij})]^{\frac{1}{2}}} \qquad (2)$$

The definition of the equivalent strain shows that the incremental effective strain $d\bar{\varepsilon}$ becomes the uniaxial strain $d\varepsilon_{11}$ under uniaxial loading conditions for incompressible materials. The incremental equivalent plastic strain $d\bar{\varepsilon}$ is similarly defined as above.

6. It can be shown that the effective strain provides an approximation to the maximum resultant shear strain. Therefore, the total effective strain, defined as $\bar{\varepsilon} = \int d\bar{\varepsilon}$, is a measure of the complete plastic loading history. Since the proportionality between $\bar{\sigma}$ and the maximum shear stress $\bar{\varepsilon}$ and that between and the maximum shear strain are similar, a representation of the stress-strain relationship in terms of $\bar{\sigma}$ and $\bar{\varepsilon}$ is nearly equivalent to one expressed in terms of the maximum shear stress and maximum shear strain. Therefore, the uniaxial test data can be used to represent the stress-strain relationship under multiaxial loading by simply substituting $\bar{\sigma}$ for σ_{11} and $\bar{\varepsilon}$ for ε_{11}.

7. As proposed above, the transition from elastic to plastic deformation occurs when the maximum resultant shear stress reaches a critical value. This critical value is the shear strength of the material, k. It needs to note that every point in the work-hardening region of the stress-strain curve is a yield point for further deformation, since a metal unloaded from a plastic state behaves elastically until the shear stress again exceeds the value it had prior to unloading . Here, these ideas will be used to develop mathematical expressions or yield criteria for the conditions of plastic yield. There are two common yield criteria for metals, one based on the maximum shear stress, and the other on the equivalent stress $\bar{\sigma}$.

8. Based on the critical shear stress concept, a yield criterion may be written in terms of the principal stresses as

$$\frac{\sigma_1 - \sigma_3}{2} = \tau_{max} = k \quad \text{(at yield)} \tag{3}$$

where σ_1 and σ_3 are the maximum and the minimum principal stresses, respectively. The yield criterion given by Eq. (3) is known as the Tresca yield criterion or the maximum shear criterion.

9. It is known that the equivalent stress $\bar{\sigma}$ is nearly equal to twice the maximum resultant shear stress under various loading conditions. Since metals deform plastically when the resultant shear stress reaches a critical value, another yield criterion may be established in terms of $\bar{\sigma}$ as

$$\bar{\sigma} = \text{constant} = 2k \text{ (at yield)} \tag{4}$$

It can be shown that the equivalent stress is related to the distortional energy stored in a. body due to shear deformation only. Therefore, the yield criterion given by Eq. (4) is known as the Von Mises yield criterion or the maximum distortion energy criterion.

10. The Tresca and Mises yield criteria may be represented graphically in principal stress space. Since the Mises yield criterion states that yielding occurs when the equivalent stress $\bar{\sigma}$ is equal to the yield strength in tension, or twice the shear yield strength, the Mises yield criterion in principal stress space is represented by a circular cylinder of radius $\sqrt{2/3}\,\bar{\sigma}$ with its axis parallel to the hydrostatic stress axis. The Tresca yield criterion can be shown to be a right hexagonal cylinder in the principal stress space with its edges coinciding with the Mises yield criterion.

11. If a state of stress is such that it lies inside the Mises cylinder or the Tresca hexagon, the deformation is purely elastic. If it lies on the yield surface, plastic deformation is initiated. If the material is rigid perfectly plastic, continuous plastic deformation can occur as long as the state of stress remains on any part of the yield surface.

12. Because the equivalent stress $\bar{\sigma}$ is not exactly equal to twice the resultant shear stress, the predictions of the Tresca and the Von Mises yield criteria do not agree everywhere, the maximum difference being about 15.5% when a simple shear stress is applied. The experimental results lie somewhere between these two criteria. Although the experimental results tend to follow the Von Mises yield criterion, the choice between the two criteria should be dictated by mathematical convenience.

New Words and Expressions

approximation [əˌprɔksi'meiʃən] n. 近似,接近
assumption [ə'sʌmpʃən] n. 假定,假设

constitutive ['kɔnstitju:tiv] *adj.* 构成的,要素的,本质的,本构的
criterion [krai'tiəriən] *n.* 标准,准则
criteria *n. pl.* 标准,准则
deviator ['di:vieitə] *n.* 偏离,偏量
dictate [dik'teit] *v.* 决定,确定;指令,指示;命令; *n.* 指示
distortion [dis'tɔ:ʃən] *n.* 扭曲,变形
equivalent [i'kwivələnt] *adj.* 相当的 *n.* 等价物
hexagon ['heksəgən] *n.* 六角形,六边形
incompressible [,inkəm'presəbl] *adj.* 不能压缩的
increment ['inkrimənt] *n.* 增量,增加
incremental [inkri'mentəl] *adj.* 增量的
invariant [in'vɛəriənt] *n.* 不变量 *adj.* 不变的
multiaxial [,mʌlti'æksiəl] *adj.* 多轴的
parameter [pə'ræmitə] *n.* 参量,参数
plastic ['plæstik, plɑ:stik] *n.* 塑料 *adj.* 塑性的
plot [plɔt] *n.* 图,标绘图,图表 *v.* 绘…的图,标绘绘图
principal ['prinsəp(ə)l,-sip-] *adj.* 主要的,首要的; *n.* 首长,校长,主犯
proportional [prə'pɔ:ʃnl] *adj.* 比例的,成比例的
proportionality [prə,pɔ:ʃə'næliti] *n.* 比例
resultant [ri'zʌltənt] *adj.* 合成的 *n.* 合力
shear [ʃiə] *n.* 剪,切,切力 *v.* 剪切
tensile ['tensail] *adj.* 拉伸的
transition [træn'ziʒən,-'siʃən] *n.* 转变,转换,过渡
uniaxial ['ju:ni'æksiəl] *adj.* 单轴的
yield [ji:ld] *v.* 屈服;产生; *n.* 产量,收益;屈服(点)

Lesson 29

Plastic Flow Rule

1. The Tresca and Mises yield criteria may be represented graphically in principal stress space. Since the Mises yield criterion states that yielding occurs when the equivalent stress $\bar{\sigma}$ is equal to the yield strength in tension, or twice the shear yield strength, the Mises yield criterion in principal stress space is represented by a circular cylinder of radius $\sqrt{2/3}\,\bar{\sigma}$ with its axis parallel to the hydrostatic stress axis. The Tresca yield criterion can be shown to be a right hexagonal cylinder in the principal stress space with its edges coinciding with the Mises yield criterion.

2. If a state of stress is such that it lies inside the Mises cylinder or the Tresca hexagon, the deformation is purely elastic. If it lies on the surface, plastic deformation is initiated. If the material is rigid perfectly plastic, continuous plastic deformation can occur as long as the state of stress remains on any part of the yield surface. If the state of stress varies such that it moves toward the inside of the surface, elastic unloading occurs. In Fig. 1, which represents a work-hardening material, the deformation from A to B can occur only if the loading changes in such a way that as the state of stress moves it will remain on the current yield surface produced by the process of work hardening.

3. The changes which occur in the yield surface due to work

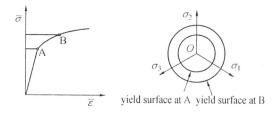

Fig. 1 Expansion of the yield surface of a work-hardening material without change of shape during plastic deformation.

hardening depend on the amount of plastic flow which has occurred and on the assumptions made about the nature of the work-hardening process. Experiments show that when yield is defined as 0.2% deviation from elastic behavior, changes in the shape of the yield surface caused by prior work harddening are quite small. Therefore, it will be assumed that the effect of work hardening is simply to enlarge the yield locus without changing its shape. This assumption is often called the isotropic work-hardening hypothesis.

4. The rate of change of the size of the yield locus with plastic strain is well defined for uniaxial tension by the tensile stress-strain curve. When the state of strain differs from this case, it is necessary to determine how much work-hardening effect the strain has. One method is to express the work-hardening effect of the plastic strain in terms of the concept of the equivalent plastic strain increment $d\bar{\varepsilon}^p$, and the equivalent plastic strain, defined by $\bar{\varepsilon}^p = \int d\bar{\varepsilon}^p$. It can then be assumed that the size of the yield locus defined by the current value of the flow stress in tension is solely a function of $\bar{\varepsilon}^p$.

5. If it is assumed that (1) the work hardening is isotropic and

(2) the size of the yield surface is a function of only the equivalent plastic strain $\bar{\varepsilon}^p$, then the conditions for plastic yield under any state of loading can be determined from the value of $\bar{\varepsilon}^p$ integrated over the deformation history of the body and the tensile stress-strain curve of the material. These assumptions predict yield stresses which agree with those found by experiment to within 10% for most metals. It should be noted that engineering materials may not be fully isotropic, independent of hydrostatic pressure, and independent of the sense of normal stresses, which are the underlying assumptions for the Tresca and Mises yield criteria.

6. The previous discussion is confined to the problem of determining which states of stress can cause plastic deformation and how they depend on the preceding plastic strain history. However, nothing has yet been said about what plastic strain increments occur when the yield condition is satisfied. It is therefore necessary to develop relationships between various stress components and various plastic strain components, similar to the generalized Hooke's laws for elastic deformation, assuming that the material behavior as characterized by the equivalent stress and the equivalent strain is known.

7. Since the plastic deformation of metals is due only to the shear stress components, and since the deviator stress represents the shear component, i.e., the distortional component of stress, it is reasonable to expect that the incremental deviatoric plastic strain is proportional to the deviator stress, i.e., $d\varepsilon_{ij}^p = \lambda \sigma_{ij}'$. The proportionality constant λ can be expressed in terms of the equivalent stress and strain by considering the special case of a tensile test. After a few mathematical manipulations, the resulting stress-strain relation for plastic deformation may be written as

$$d\varepsilon_{ij}^p = \frac{3}{2}\frac{d\overline{\varepsilon}^P}{2\overline{\sigma}}\sigma_{ij}' \qquad (1)$$

Eq. (1) is known as the Prandtl-Reuss equation or the proportionality flow rule.

8. The constitutive relations descussed for the plastic case may be summarized by comparing them with those of the elastic case. In the elastic case, the constitutive relation is completely described by Hooke's law, with two elastic constants, e. g., elastic modulus E and Poisson' ratio υ, to characterize the material properties. In the plastic case, the flow rule, such as the Prandtl-Reuss equation, substitutes for Hooke's law in the elastic case, and a work-hardening relationship, such as $\overline{\sigma} = C(\overline{\varepsilon}^p)^n$ is used to characterize the material properties. The constant of proportionality in Eq. (1), $\lambda = 3/2d\overline{\varepsilon}^p/\overline{\sigma}$, is equivalent to the proportionality constant for elastic distortion, $1/2G$, except that λ is a function of strain.

New Words and Expressions

assumption [ə'sʌmpʃən] n. 假定,设想,担任,承当
characterize ['kæriktəraiz] vt. 表现…的特色,表征
coincide [ˌkəuin'said] vi. 一致,符合
confine ['kɔnfain] vt. 限制,禁闭; n. 界限,边界
constant ['kɔnstənt] n. [数、物]常数,恒量; adj. 不变的,持续的
constitutive ['kɔnstitjuːtiv] adj. 构成的,本构的,制定的
continuous [kən'tinjuəs] adj. 连续的,持续的
criterion [krai'tiəriən] n. 标准,准则,准据,规范
cylinder ['silində] n. 圆筒,圆柱体,汽缸,柱面
deformation [ˌdiːfɔː'meiʃən] n. 变形,畸形
deviation [ˌdiːvi'eiʃən] n. 背离

deviator ['di:vieitə] n. 偏量；偏差器，变向装置
deviatoric adj. 偏的，偏量的
distortion [dis'tɔ:ʃən] n. 扭曲，歪曲，(信号等的)失真，畸变，曲解
equivalent [i'kwivələnt:] adj. 相等的，相当的；n. 等价物，相等物
flow [fləu] n. 流程，流动 vi. 流动
function ['fʌŋkʃən] n. 功能，作用，职责，[数]函数
generalize ['dʒenərəlaiz] vt. 归纳，概括，推广
graphical ['græfikəl] adj. 图形的，绘画的
harden ['hɑ:dn] vt. 使变硬，使坚强；vi. 变硬，硬化
hexagon ['heksəgən] n. 六角形，六边形
hexagonal [hek'sægənəl] adj. 六角形的，六边形的
hydrostatic [ˌhaidrəu'stætik] adj. 静水力学的，流体静力学的
hypothesis [hai'pɔθisis] n. 假设
increment ['inkrimənt] n. 增加，增量
incremental [inkri'mentəl] adj. 增加的，增量的
initiate [i'niʃieit] vt. 开始，发动；v. 开始，发起
integrate ['intigreit] vt. 求……的积分，使成整体，使一体化
　　　　　　　v. 结合
isotropic [aisəu'trɔpik] adj. 各向同性的，等方向性的
locus ['ləukəs] n. 地点，所在地，[数]轨迹
manipulation [məˌnipju'leiʃən] n. 处理，操作，运算，操纵
normal ['nɔ:məl] n. 正规，常态，[数]法线；adj. 正常的，标准的
parallel ['pærəlel] adj. 平行的，类似的；n. 平行线，相似物
plastic ['plæstik, plɑ:stik] n. 塑料，塑料制品；adj. 塑性的
preceding [pri(:)'si:diŋ] adj. 在前的，前述的
pressure ['preʃə(r)] n. 压，压力，压迫，强制，紧迫
principal ['prinsəp(ə)l, -sip-] adj. 主要的，首要的；n. 负责
　　　　　　　人，首长，校长，主犯
proportional [prə'pɔ:ʃənl] adj. 比例的，成比例的，均衡的

proportionality [prəˌpɔːʃə'næliti] *n*. 比例(性);均衡(性);相称
radius ['reidjəs] *n*. 半径,范围
remain [ri'mein] *vi*. 保持,逗留,剩余,残存
rigid ['ridʒid] *adj*. 刚硬的,刚性的,严格的
rule [ruːl] *n*. 规则,章程,准则; *vt*. 规定,统治; *vi*. 统治,裁定
summarize ['sʌməraiz] *v*. 概述,总结
uniaxial ['juːni'æksiəl] *adj*. 单轴的
yield [jiːld] *n*. 产量,屈服; *v*. 出产,生产; *vi*.(~ to)屈服,屈从

Lesson 30

Plastic Limit Analysis

1. When the extent of plastic deformation is small, both elastic and plastic deformations may have to be considered simultaneously in the analysis. Some of the numerous elastoplastic problems include the bending of sheets and beams, the deformation of vessels, the propagation of cracks in metals, the torsion of bars, and the rolling of sheets. The mathematical difficulties multiply rapidly in comparison with pure elastic or fully plastic case, and the available solutions are generally limited to the simpler problems.

2. When the magnitude of plastic deformation is larger than the elastic strain by an order of magnitude or more, and if the particular phenomenon of interest is largely controlled by the plastic deformation, the elastic deformation may be neglected. The solution to many physical problems becomes much easier when this can be done. Some of the commonly used solutions are energy method, the uniform stress method, slip line solutions and the plastic limit analysis. Among them, the plastic limit analysis is relatively easy to carry out and thus is very useful.

3. In theory, to obtain a solution of a problem involving plastic deformation, the entire deformation history must be traced. The solution is often complicated because accurate constitutive

relations for real materials are highly intractable mathematically, and even using the idealized constitutive relations, exact solutions to many real problems are difficult to obtain. Furthermore, in many practical applications, such as wire and cup drawing, the complete history of deformation is not required, and only the limiting load is of interest. Therefore, it will be very desirable to have a technique which approximates limiting solutions in a simple manner and at the same time sets bounds on the degree of approximation involved.

4. One of the most useful approximate methods, which is based on the theorems of limit analysis, can be used to obtain an approximation to the limiting load which a structure can carry out. The limiting solutions are obtained in the form of the upper and lower bounds on the limit load. An upper-bound solution overestimates the true load while a lower-bound solution underestimated it. If both the upper and lower bounds can be established the range of the true load is determined. The smaller the difference between the upper- and the lower-bound solutions, the closer is the approximation to the exact value.

5. Although it is not always possible to determine both the upper-bound and lower-bound solutions, any limiting solution can be useful in a proper context. For example, in the materials processing field, the upper-bound solution can provide answers for stress which will be more than sufficient to perform a given task. On the other hand, in structural designs, the lower-bound solutions can provide a conservative estimate of the load-carrying capacity of a structure, and is thus much more desirable than the overestimated upper-bound.

6. The theorems of limit analysis are developed for rigid-

plastic materials. These theorems are similar to the theorem of minimum potential energy and the theorem of minimum complementary energy in elasticity. The limit theorems provide the basis for determining limiting solutions which can be classified into upper-bound and lower-bound solutions. The upper- and lower-bound theorems will be simply stated as follows.

7. The Lower-Bound Theorem: The load corresponding to an assumed stress field which satisfies

   (1) the equilibrium condition everywhere in the continuum
   (2) the yield condition
   (3) the stress boundary conditions

is always less than that corresponding to the true stress field. Therefore, the lower-bound to the limit load can be obtained by assuming a stress field which satisfies the above three conditions, totally neglecting the geometric compatibility condition.

8. The Upper-Bound Theorem: The actual work done in deforming a rigid-plastic continuum is always less than the work done by an assumed displacement which

   (1) satisfies the displacement boundary condition
   (2) yields a strain field which satisfies the incompressibility condition.

Therefore, the upper bound to the limit load can be obtained by assuming a displacement field which satisfies the above two conditions and by equating the work done by the external agent with that done deforming the material along the assumed displacement field. The equilibrium condition is totally neglected in obtaining the upper-bound solution.

9. In summary, to obtain an exact solution in continuum mechanics, three basic conditions must be satisfied, i.e., the

equilibrium equations, the geometric compatibility, and the constitutive relationships of the continuum. The solutions obtained without satisfying all these conditions are, therefore, called approximate solutions. Plastic limit analysis is one of the most commonly used approximate solutions. It is a very powerful and useful tool for mechanical engineers.

New Words and Expressions

agent ['eidʒənt] n. 代理(商)
approximate [ə'prɔksimeit] adj. 近似的,大约的; v. 近似,接近,接近,约计
bend [bend] [bend] v. 弯曲,屈服; n. 弯曲
bound [baund] [baund] n. 范围,限度,跃进,跳; adj. 被束缚的,装订的; v. 跳跃,限制
capacity [kə'pæsiti] n. 容量,能力,接受力,地位
classify ['klæsifai] vt. 分类,分等
compatibility [kəmˌpæti'biliti] n. 协调(性),相容(性)
complementary [kɔmplə'mentəri] adj. 补充的,补足的
conservative [kən'sə:vətiv] adj. 保守的,守旧的
constitutive ['kɔnstitjuːtiv] adj. 构成的,本构的;制定的
crack [kræk] n. 裂缝,噼啪声; v. (使)破裂,(使)爆裂
draw [drɔː] v. 拉,曳,牵,画,绘制,拖曳,领取,提取
equilibrium [ˌiːkwi'libriəm] n. 平衡,均衡
incompressibility [inkəmpresə'biliti] n. 不可压缩性
intractable [in'træktəbl] adj. 难处理的
involve [in'vɔlv] vt. 包括,包括,笼罩,潜心于
limit ['limit] n. 界限,限度; vt. 限制,限定
minimum ['miniməm] adj. 最小的,最低的; n. 最小值,最小化
multiply ['mʌltipli] v. 乘,增加

neglect [ni'glekt] *vt*. 忽视,疏忽,漏做; *n*. 忽视,疏忽,漏做
order ['ɔ:də] *n*. 次序,秩序,命令,定单; *vt*. 命令,定购,定制
phenomenon [fi'nɔminən] *n*. 现象
plastic ['plæstik, plɑ:stik] *n*. 塑胶,塑料; *adj*. 塑胶的,塑性的
potential [pə'tenʃ(ə)l] *adj*. 潜在的,势的,位的; *n*. 潜能,潜力
process [prɔ'ses] *n*. 过程,方法,程序,步骤; *vt*. 加工,处理
propagation [ˌprɔpə'geiʃən] *n*. (声波,电磁辐射等)传播;(动植物)繁殖
rigid ['ridʒid] *adj*. 刚硬的,刚性的,严格的
roll [rəul] *vt*. 辗,轧; *n*. (一)卷,摆动,名单
sheet [ʃi:t] *n*. (一)片,(一)张,薄片,被单
simultaneously [siməl'teiniəsly;(us)saim-:] *adv*. 同时地,同时发生地
slip [slip] *n*. 滑倒,滑移,片,纸片; *vi*. 滑动; *vt*. 使滑动; *adj*. 滑动的
theorem ['θiərəm] *n*. 定理,法则
torsion ['tɔ:ʃən] *n*. [物][机] 扭转,转矩
trace [treis] *n*. 痕迹,踪迹,微量; *vt*. 描绘,追踪,探索
vessel ['vesl] *n*. 船,容器,器皿
wire ['waiə] *n*. 金属丝,电线; *vt*. 布线,给…装电线,用电线连接

Lesson 31

Mechanisms of Elastic Deformation

1. When one comes to deal with engineering materials, he is introduced to what at first appear to be a multitude of diverse subjects. Unlike the courses of statics, dynamics or structural mechanics, the subject of the mechanical behavior of solids cannot be arranged and presented as a logically unified scheme, since our modern understanding of the theory is as yet incomplete. However, after a period of struggle, the bewildered student will find that there is after all an underlying order that ties all engineering materials together.

2. The central unifying scheme for engineering materials would by logic seem to be the arrangement of the constituent atoms, the bond strength between them, and their interactions with other atomic species. Indeed, broad categorization of materials can actually be made on this basis. For example, it is known that metals with high melting points generally also have high yield strengths, that metals with a body-centered cubic structure are more difficult to deform than face-centered cubic metals, and that metallic elements with similar atomic radii can be combined to form alloys.

3. In discussing the mechanical behavior of materials, it is reasonable to begin with the subject of elastic behavior. Elastic

deformation arises from the small shifts in the equilibrium positions of atoms which occur when external forces are applied to a solid body, it is therefore a fundamental property of solids which can be related directly to the binding forces between atoms. Elastic deformation is homogeneous on a finer scale than other types of deformation, since it involves shifts in all of the atomic positions, not just in the positions of certain critically located atoms.

4. Because of this intrinsic nature of elastic deflections, several properties of elastic behavior can be directly deduced. Elastic deformation is completely reversible, since elastic distortions involve small-scale shifts in the equilibrium positions of the atoms, without wholesale rearrangement of the atomic positions. Removal of an applied load causes the inter-atomic potentials to return to their original state, with the result that the atoms return to their undisturbed positions, and the body returns to its original shape.

5. Because elastic deformation involves all of the atoms in the body, small changes in composition do not have a very large effect on the elastic response of the material. The exchange of a few atoms of one element for a few atoms of another in a solid changes the atomic binding forces only in the region of the atoms exchanged. The size of the effect on the elastic response of the material is roughly proportional to the number of substituted atoms and the difference in the involved binding forces. For the types of elements which are generally used in alloying, or accidentally introduced as impurities, the variation is usually only a few percent. Accordingly, the differences in elastic response among the various alloys and purities of a material are generally also a few percent. For example, nearly all of the steel alloys have a

practically identical Young's modulus of 28 to 29×10^6 psi.

6. For reasons similar to those discussed in connection with changes in composition, the elastic behavior of the material is only very slightly affected by the previous history of the material. Since elasticity is directly related to the binding between atoms, any processing which results in a material with the same crystal structure will give a material with the same elastic behavior. For example, a metal may be subjected to a number of different heat treatments which can have a profound effect on other mechanical properties. As a rule, heat treatments affect the distribution of phases in a material, but they do not alter the identity of these phases. Since the phases retain their identity, the atomic binding forces remain essentially the same, and the elastic behavior of the material undergoes no change.

7. Elastic behavior is similarly unaffected by prior deformation history, except when there has been a major realignment of the material. In crystalline materials, permanent deformation occurs via the mechanism of dislocation motion. It is possible through deformation to increase the number of dislocations in a body by many orders of magnitude. However, even in the most heavily cold-worked material, the number of atoms adjacent to defects such as dislocations, and thus able to have their binding energies significantly disturbed, are but a small percentage of the total. Since the elastic properties of the body are predominantly determined by the great mass of undisturbed material, they therefore remain unchanged.

8. Prior deformation can have a significant effect on the elastic properties of a material, if some fundamental change in the structure of the material has occurred. This would be the case, for

example, in a drawn polymer which has been sufficiently stretched to align most of the molecules in a single direction. The elastic properties of the structure are then said to be anisotropic, that is, they depend upon direction. Along the drawing axis, the elasticity will be primarily a function of the binding forces between atoms of the same molecule, while in directions perpendicular to that axis they will depend on forces between atoms of different molecules. In contrast, the elastic properties of the undrawn, unoriented polymer represent averages of the properties derived from these two different inter-atomic forces.

New Words and Expressions

align [ə'lain] v. 排列,校正
alignment [ə'lainmənt] n. 排列;校准;调整;队列
alloy ['ælɔi] n. 合金
alter ['ɔ:ltə] v. 改变
anisotropic [ə,naisəu'trɔpik] adj. 各向异性的
bewilder [bi'wildə] vt. 使迷惑
bond [bɔnd] n. 结合(物),粘结(剂),联结,合同; v. 结合,粘合;键
category ['kætigəri] n. 种类,部属;类目,范畴
composition [kɔmpə'ziʃən] n. 组成,成分,合成物
constituent [kən'stitjuənt] adj. 构成的;组成的; n. 要素;组分
crystalline ['kristəlain] adj. 结晶性的
deflection [di'flekʃən] n. 挠度,偏向
dislocation [,dislə'keiʃən] n. 位错;脱臼;转位
distortion [dis'tɔ:ʃən] n. 扭曲,变形
diverse [dai'və:s] adj. 不同的,变化多的
draw [drɔ:] v. 拉,拔出;画
dynamics [dai'næmiks] n. 动力学

identity [ai'dentiti] n. 相同,恒等式;身份
impurity [im'pjuəriti] n. 杂质,不纯
interaction [ˌintər'ækʃən] n. 交互作用
intrinsic [in'trinsik] adj. 本质的,原有的
mechanism ['mekənizəm] n. 机构;机制,机理
melt [melt] n. 熔化;v.(使)熔化
molecule ['mɔlikjuːl,'məu-] n. [化]分子
multitude ['mʌltitjuːd] n. 大量,许多;集,组
polymer ['pɔlimə] n. 聚合物
profound [prə'faund] adj. 极深的,渊博的
radii ['reidiai] n. pl. 半径
reversible [ri'vəːsəbl] adj. 可逆的,可恢复的
shift [ʃift] n. 移动,轮班,移位;vt. 替换,转移
　　vi. 转换,移动,转变
species ['spiːʃiz] n. 种,类
statics ['stætiks] n. 静力学
substitute ['sʌbstitjuːt] v. 替代;n. 代用品
underlying ['ʌndəˌlaiiŋ] adj. 在下面的
variation [ˌvɛəri'eiʃən] n. 变化,改变;变分

Lesson 32

Mechanisms of Plastic Deformation

1. The fact that metals can deform permanently upon loading after a certain initial elastic deformation is well known. The time-independent permanent deformation is defined as a plastic deformation. The purpose of the following discussion is to give the reader an understanding of the underlying physical mechanisms which are responsible for plastic behavior. In order to develop physical insights into the mechanics of plastic deformation, the nature of plastic deformation processes will be studied in terms of the microscopic behavior of metals based on dislocation theory.

2. Several interesting differences between elastic and plastic deformation should be noted. As discussed before for metals, the elastic deformation, which occurs as soon as any load is applied, involves only the stretching of atomic bonds and is a reversible process, i.e., the work done in deforming the body can be completely recovered by unloading the body. Upon unloading, the state of the metal, which may be defined in terms of the stress, the strain, and the temperature, returns to its original configuration. Furthermore, the state of an elastic solid can always be uniquely defined when two of the variables, e.g., strain and temperature, are known, regardless of the particular path of loading.

3. Plastic deformation is a permanent change in atomic positions. This occurs when one layer of atoms slips over the adjacent layer in such a way that an atom moves from its initial position to an equivalent adjacent position. When slip occurs, two planes of atoms are sheared relative to each other. The atoms are first displaced from their equilibrium positions elastically. At some point the resistance to displacement reaches a maximum, and then drops to zero. Finally, the atoms are again in equilibrium but displaced by a certain distance from their initial positions. Such a shift can occur whenever the shear stress on a plane in the body reaches a critical value. Obviously, the force resisting this shearing process has a periodic nature as slipping proceeds.

4. Unlike elastic deformation, plastic deformation is very sensitive to discrete defects in the material. If the slipping process can be stopped completely at one point on a plane in the body, a large portion of the plane can be kept from slipping. The stress necessary to cause plastic deformation is therefore quite sensitive to localized irregularities in the material, such as crystal lattice defects, impurity atoms, second-phase particles, and grain boundaries. The plastic properties of the material are, for this reason, much more strongly affected by composition and prior history than is the elastic behavior.

5. During deformation, defects, primarily dislocations, accumulate in the lattice structure of the material and inhibit the slipping process. This causes an increase in the stress required for continuous deformation. In plasticity, this phenomenon is referred to as work hardening. The flow stress of metals can be increased by such metallurgical means as alloying and inclusion of secondary phase particles. The strengthening mechanisms involve either

introduction of physical obstacles to dislocation motion or creation of internal stress fields.

6. Alloying, which is called solution hardening, creates internal stress fields by replacing the original atoms with other atoms of different sizes and by inserting small nonmetallic atoms in interstitial sites. In substitutional alloying, foreign atoms whose atomic radii are within 15% of the host atoms are mixed with the latter. These atoms occupy regular lattice sites and create internal stress fields due to the difference in the atomic radii. When such metals are plastically deformed, the dislocation motion is impeded by the internal stress field. Therefore, a greater external stress must be applied to deform the metal plastically than when it is free of foreign atoms.

7. Secondary-phase particles are incorporated by either precipitation of secondary phases during cooling and aging or by inclusion of insoluble secondary-phase particles during the melting process. In any two-phase material where the second phase exists as a dispersion of fine particles in a matrix of the major phase, dislocation motion is impeded. The origin of the resisting force depends on the materials in question. In some cases, the particles are a hard, brittle, nonmetallic phase which cannot be sheared. Therefore, the dislocations cannot pass through the particles but must surround the particles.

8. Plastic deformation is not reversible. During plastic deformation the equilibrium position of the atoms is permanently changed. Also, plastic deformation depends on loading history, because the structure of the material changes continuously during the deformation. Consequently, the plastic state of a metal cannot be defined uniquely in terms of the stress, the current strain, and

the temperature.

9. The non-uniqueness of the plastic state and the dependence of plastic deformation on the loading path imply that it is no longer possible to determine the total plastic strain from the state of stress and the temperature, whereas in the elastic case, the total strain is directly related to these two variables. Therefore, in plasticity it is necessary to deal with incremental deformation at a given state of loading and obtain the total plastic deformation by summing up all of the incremental loading.

New Words and Expressions

accumulate [ə'kju:mjuleit] v. 积聚, 堆积, 累积
adjacent [ə'dʒeisənt] *adj*. 邻近的, 连接的
age [eidʒ] n. 年龄, 时代; v. 老化, 陈化, 时效
configuration [kən,figju'reiʃən] n. 构形, 结构, 构造
defect [di'fekt] n. 缺点, 缺陷
discrete [dis'kri:t] *adj*. 离散的, 不连续的
dislocation [,dislə'keiʃən] n. 位错, 脱臼
dispersion [dis'pə:ʃən] n. 散布, 弥[扩, 耗]散; 散射
grain [grein] n. 颗粒, 晶粒
impede [im'pi:d] vt. 阻碍, 阻止; 阻抗
impurity [im'pjuəriti] n. 杂质; 不纯
incremental [inkri'mentəl] *adj*. 增量的, 增加的
inhibit [in'hibit] v. 抑制, 禁止
insoluble [in'sɔljubl] *adj*. 不能溶解的
interstitial [,intə(:)'stiʃəl] *adj*. 空隙的, 裂缝的
involve [in'vɔlv] vt. 包括, 涉及, 使陷于
lattice ['lætis] n. 格子, 晶格
layer ['leiə] n. 层

metallurgy [me'tælədʒi] n. 冶金(学)
obstacle ['ɔbstəkl] n. 障碍,妨害物
periodic [piəri'ɔdik] adj. 周期的,循环的
permanent ['pə:mənənt] adj. 永久的,固定的
precipitation [pri͵sipi'teiʃən] n. 沉淀,析出
resistance [ri'zistəns] n. 抵抗力,阻力;电阻;反抗
responsible [ris'pɔnsəbl] adj. 有责任的;应负责任的(to sb.; for sth.)
be responsible for 导致,引起,是(造成)…的(主要)原因
reversible [ri'və:səbl] adj. 可逆的,可恢复的
sensitive ['sensitiv] adj. 敏感的,灵敏的
shift [ʃift] n. 移动,移位,轮班; vt. 替换,转移,改变,移转; vi. 转换,移动,转变
slip [slip] n. 滑移,滑动; vi. 滑,滑动; vt. (使)滑动
stretch [stretʃ] v. 伸展,伸缩
substitution [͵sʌbsti'tju:ʃən] n. 替换,代替物
sum [sʌm] n. 总数,和;金额;概要; v. 总计,合计;概略,概括
variable ['vɛəriəbl] n. 变量; adj. 可变的,变量的

Lesson 33

Finite Element Method

1. The finite element method is a numerical method which can be used for the accurate solution of complex engineering problems. The method was first developed in 1956 by Turner, Clough, Martin and Topp for the analysis of aircraft structural problems. Over the years, the finite element technique has been so well established that today it is considered to be one of the best methods for solving a wide variety of practical problems efficiently. One of the main reasons for the popularity of the method is that once a general computer program is written, it can be used for the solution of any problem by simply changing the input data.

2. In the finite element method, the actual continuum or body of matter like solid, liquid or gas is represented as an assemblage of subdivisions called finite elements. These elements are considered to be interconnected at specified joints which are called nodes or nodal points. The nodes usually lie on the element boundaries where adjacent elements are considered to be connected.

3. Since the actual variation of the field variable such as displacement, stress, temperature, pressure or velocity, inside the continuum is not known, we assume that the variation of the

field variable inside a finite element can be approximated by a simple function. These approximating functions, which are also called interpolation models, are defined in terms of the values of the field variables at the nodes.

4. When field equations, e.g., the equilibrium equations for the whole continuum are written, the new unknowns will be the nodal values of the field variable. By solving the field equations, which are generally in the form of matrix equations, the nodal values of the field variable will be known. Once these are known, the approximating functions will define the field variable throughout the assemblage of elements. The solution of a general continuum problem by the finite element method always follows an orderly step-by-step process. With reference to static structural problems, the step-by-step procedure can be stated as follows:

5. **Step 1**: *Discretization of the structure*

The first step in the finite element method is to divide the structure or solution region into subdivisions or elements. Hence the structure that is being analyzed has to be modeled with suitable finite elements. The number, type, size and arrangement of the elements have to be decided.

6. **Step 2**: *Selection of a proper displacement model*

Since the displacement solution of a complex structure under any specified load conditions cannot be predicted exactly, we assume some suitable solution within an element to approximate the unknown solution. The assumed solution must be simple from computational point of view, but it should satisfy certain convergence requirements. In general, the solution or the interpolation model is taken in the form of a polynomial.

7. **Step 3**: *Derivation of element stiffness matrices and load vectors*

From the assumed displacement model, the stiffness matrix $[K]^e$ and the load vector $\{p\}^e$, of element 'e' are to be derived by using either equilibrium conditions or a suitable variational principle.

8. **Step 4**: *Assemblage of the overall equilibrium equations*

Since the structure is composed of several finite elements, the individual element stiffness matrices and load vectors are to be assembled in a suitable manner and the overall equilibrium equations have to be formulated as

$$[K]\{u\} = \{p\} \qquad (1)$$

where $[K]$ is called the assembled stiffness matrix, $\{u\}$ is the vector of nodal displacements and $\{p\}$ is the vector of nodal forces for the complete structure.

9. **Step 5**: *Solution for the unknown nodal displacements*

The overall equilibrium equations have to be modified to account for the boundary conditions of the problem. After the incorporation of the boundary conditions, the equilibrium equations can be solved by using a standard computer subroutine. For linear problems, the vector $\{u\}$ can be solved very easily. But for nonlinear problems, the solution has to be obtained in a sequence of steps, each step involving the modification of the stiffness matrix $[K]$ and/or the load vector $\{p\}$.

10. **Step 6**: *Computation of element strains and stresses*

After solution of the finite element equations, form the known nodal displacements $\{u\}$, if required. Finally the element strains and stresses can be computed by using the necessary equations of solid or structural mechanics.

11. The finite element method has developed originally for the analysis of structural mechanics. However, the general nature of

its theory makes it applicable to a wide variety of boundary value problems in engineering. A boundary value problem is one in which a solution is sought in the domain of a body subject to the satisfaction of prescribed boundary conditions on the dependent variables or their derivatives.

12. The general applicability of the finite element method can be seen by observing the strong similarities that exist between various types of engineering problems. In summary, the applications of the finite element method can be classified into three major categories of boundary value problems, namely,

(i) equilibrium or steady state or time independent problems,

(ii) eigenvalue problems,

(iii) propagation or transient problems.

New Words and Expressions

approximate [ə'prɔksimeit] *adj.* 近似的, 大约的; *vt.* 使接近, 粗略估计
assemblage [ə'semblidʒ] *n.* 集合, 装配
boundary ['baundəri] *n.* 边界, 分界线
category ['kætigəri] *n.* 种类; 项目
continuum [kən'tinjuəm] *n.* 连续体, 连续统
convergence [kən'və:dʒəns] *n.* 收敛
discretization [dis̩kri:ti'zeiʃən] *n.* 离散, [数]离散化
displacement [dis'pleismənt] *n.* 位移, 换置
domain [dəu'mein] *n.* 领域, 范围; 领土
eigenvalue [aigən̩vælju:] *n.* [数.物]特征值
element ['elimənt] *n.* 单元, 元素, 要素, 成分
equilibrium [ˌi:kwi'libriəm] *n.* 平衡, 均衡

field [fi:ld] n. 场，域，领域
finite ['fainait] adj. 有限的，有穷的
incorporation [in,kɔ:pə'reiʃən] n. 结合；包含；编入
interconnect [,intə(:)kə'nekt] vt. 使互相连接
interpolation [in,tə:pou'leiʃən] n. 插入[值]，内插；插补；插值法，内插[推]法
matrix ['meitriks] n. 矩阵；基体
nodal ['nəudəl] adj. 结点的，节的
node [nəud] n. 结节，节
numerical [nju(:)'merikəl] adj. 数值的，数字的
polynomial [,pɔli'nəumjəl] adj. [数]多项式的；n. 多项式
principle ['prinsəpl] n. 原理
propagation [,prɔpə'geiʃən] n. 传播，繁殖
requirement [ri'kwaiəmənt] n. 必要条件，需求
solid ['sɔlid] adj. 固体的，坚硬的，稳固的
steady ['stedi] adj. 稳定的，稳态的
stiffness ['stifnis] n. 刚度，坚硬
subdivision ['sʌbdi,viʒən] n. 细分，分部
subroutine [,sʌbru:'ti:n] n. 子程序
transient ['trænziənt] adj. 瞬变的，瞬态的
variable ['vɛəriəbl] n. 变量，可变量
variation [,vɛəri'eiʃən] n. 变化，变更
variational [,vɛəri'eiʃənəl] adj. 变化的；变分的
vector ['vektə] n. 矢量

Lesson 34

Programming A Problem Solution

1. The *finite element method* is essentially a process through which a continuum with infinite degrees of freedom can be approximated to be an assemblage of sub-regions each with a specified but now finite number of unknowns. The sub-regions are defined as elements and each such element interconnects with others in a way familiar to engineers dealing with discrete structural or electrical assemblies. The finite element method has now become recognized as a general method of wide applicability to various engineering and physical science problems. The real application of finite element methods requires not only the mastery of the theory but also a considerable computer programming effort.

2. Starting at the element level, the behavior of each element is described mathematically in terms of element matrices. The global behavior is then obtained by superposition of the element matrices and expressed in terms of global matrix, which represents the governing system of equations. The matrix operations involved in a finite element solution, such as the matrix inversion, eigenvalue and eigenvector calculations, and the solution of a system of equations, are ideally suited for computer automation. The practical application of the finite element method

is feasible only if electronic computers are used and all the computations are expressed in matrix form.

3. The first step in programming the solution of a problem is to make an analysis in detail and select an appropriate solution scheme. Then a computer solution procedure to be implemented is schematized graphically, by means of a diagram called flow-chart. These diagrams can be detailed to a greater or lesser extent, according to certain circumstances, but they must be fundamental to the analysis and understanding of all aspects of the computer solution. Once the flow chart is completed, the computer solution can be coded, writing the computer program by using a computer language selected. This work is usually carried out by a programmer.

4. With the program registered in some information support, and the data and proper control commands added, the program is ready to be tested by submitting it for processing. At the beginning, the program will include some errors that may be syntax errors and logic errors. Syntax errors appear because some of the rules of the language are violated. Normally these can be easily detected and corrected. Logic errors correspond to the case that a syntax error-free program is submitted for execution, but it does not produce the desired results.

5. The following situations can be encountered during processing a computer program.

  (1) Execution of the program stops before producing any results.

  (2) Execution of the program does not stop and results are not produced. The program is finally discontinued after exceeding the allowed time limit.

(3) Results are produced, but they are incorrect.

(4) The program works successfully.

6. In the first processing of a program it is very rare to have the situation (4). In the other cases, the programmer will have to make a careful examination to detect and correct the existing errors, referred to as bugs. This task is usually called debugging the program. It is important to note that a good programmer is not the one who transforms the definition of the problem into a program the quickest, but the one who is fastest in having the program working properly. Debugging can be simplified by a careful selection of the test data. These should not be chosen arbitrarily. It is better to use the test data for which results are available, starting with simple cases, but finally testing all the possible alternatives. Also it is very helpful to include in the program statements for the intermediate output. These will indicate where the computation is going wrong. When the program is correct these statements can be removed.

7. Once the program is working, it can be used to solve practical problems. Even then the user should not accept the results blindly. Consistency checks should be performed on the results to evaluate their correctness. Many times they will be found to be incorrect because the data was specified erroneously. It is also possible that the programmer declared the program to be correct after a few tests, whthout checking all the alternatives. Sometimes the user is working with a large general programming system. The implementation of these general systems can be so complicated, and the tests required so extensive, that they are rarely 'bug-free'. In all cases the user should never accept the correctness of computer results, until after analysing them and

being reasonably sure that they are not erroneous.

8. There is no definite rule, which can be generally used to determine the number of elements used in a finite element mesh in order to evaluate the accuracy of the solution obtained. This question has no easy answer, since it depends both on the type of problem, and on the type of element used. In practice, a problem can be solved with several different meshes, with increasing number of elements and nodal points, and the comparison of the numerical solution obtained can help in evaluating approximately the precision achieved.

9. The formulation of a finite element problem is made in terms of some problem variables, which are taken as the basic unknowns. Once the system of equations is solved, we obtain the values of those basic unknowns. However, the knowledge of the values of other variables may be even more important than those of the basic unknowns. For instance, in a fluid flow problem the solution can be formulated in terms of the stream lines, but we might be interested in knowing the flow velocities. In a solid mechanics problem we can take the displacements as basic unknowns, but we will also be interested in knowing the stresses. Therefore, once the system of equations is solved, it is often necessary to compute the secondary results that may be of interest for deep understanding of the problem.

New Words and Expressions

alternative [ɔːlˈtɔːnətiv] *n*. 二中择一; *adj*. 选择性的
approximate [əˈprɔksimeit] *adj*. 近似的,大约的; *v*. 近似
assembly [əˈsembli] *n*. 集合,装配,集会,汇编
blindly [ˈblaindli] *adv*. 盲目地,摸索地

bug [bʌg] n. 小虫,臭虫;程序代码
chart [tʃɑːt] n. 海图; vt. 制图
code [kəud] n. 代码; v. 编码
continuous [kən'tinjuəs] adj. 连续的,持续的
debug [diː'bʌg] vt. <俗> 除错; v. 调试,[计]调试工具
derivative [di'rivətiv] adj. 引出的; n. 导数,微商,派生的事物,派生词
discrete [dis'kriːt] adj. 不连续的,离散的
domain [dəu'mein] n. 领土,领地,范围,领域
eigenvalue [aigən͵vælju:] n. [数.物]特征值
eigenvector [aigən͵vektə(r)] n. [数]特征向量
erroneous [i'rəunjəs] adj. 错误的,不正确的
execution [͵eksi'kjuːʃən] n. 实行,完成,执行
finite ['fainait] adj. 有限的
element ['elimənt] n. 要素,元素
flow-chart n. 流程框图
functional ['fʌŋkʃənl] adj. 功能的;函数的,泛函(数)的
govern ['gʌvən] v. 统治,管理
imply [im'plai] vt. 暗示,意味
infinitesimal [in͵finə'tesiməl] adj. 无穷小的; n. 极小量
integration [͵inti'greiʃən] n. 综合;积分
inversion [in'vəːʃən] n. 倒置
mastery ['mɑːstəri] n. 掌握
matrix ['meitriks] n. 矩阵
mesh [meʃ] n. 网孔,圈套,陷阱
order ['ɔːdə] n. 次序; vt. 命令
procedure [prə'siːdʒə] n. 程序,过程
program ['prəugræm:] n. 节目,程序; vt. 规划
programmer ['prəugræmə] n. 程序师,程序规划员

region [ˈriːdʒən] n. 区域
register [ˈredʒistə] n. 记录；vt. 记录；vi. 登记
schematize [ˈskiːmətaiz] vt. 把…系统化,用计划表达
stream [striːm] n. 溪；v. 流
subdivide [ˈsʌbdiˈvaid] v. 再分,细分
submit [səbˈmit] v. (使)服从；vt. 提交,递交
superposition [ˌsjuːpəpəˈziʃən] n. 重叠,重合,叠合
syntax [ˈsintæks] n. [语]语法,有秩序的排列,句子构造,句法
variable [ˈvɛəriəbl] n. [数]变量；adj. 可变的

Lesson 35

Experimental Techniques

1. The experimental techniques currently used in structural mechanics may be divided into two broad groups, which are the *whole field methods and the point-by-point methods*. In the *whole field methods*, the strains or displacements are measured over a certain area, while in *point-by-point methods* they are measured at selected positions.

2. **The whole field methods**

(a) *Grid method*. A grid is inscribed on the unloaded component or model and the displacements of the nodal points upon loading are measured, usually from photographs taken first in the unloaded and then in the loaded positions. Only large deformations, as occur in the plastic field or when the material creeps can be determined.

3. (b) *Brittle coatings*. The structural component is painted with a lacquer, which forms a brittle coating when it dries. Upon straining, the coating cracks along lines approximately perpendicular to the direction of the maximum tensile strain. The method is best suited for qualitative analysis since its accuracy is affected by small variations in the temperature, humidity, and other variables beyond the control of the experimentalist.

4. (c) *Moire fringes*. A grating consisting of equidistant

parallel bars and slits of pitch is fixed to the surface of a component and an identical reference grating is either placed or projected on the surface. If the reference and model gratings are parallel, and the bars in both coincide, dark bands appear when the model grating is strained in the direction perpendicular to that of the bars. These dark bands correspond to those positions where the slits of the reference grating are obscured by bars in the strained model grating.

5. (d) *Interferometers and laser holograms*. A pattern, called a hologram, is reproduced on a photographic plate, and represents the interference between light reflected by the deformed body and a reference beam from the source itself. While it is not possible to visualize the object by simply looking at the hologram, a true three-dimensional image is obtained when the hologram is viewed with the same light source that was used for its production, or with any other monochromatic source. The hologram constitutes a permanent true record of the deformation of the model under load.

6. (e) *Photoelasticity*. Many non-crystalline transparent materials that are optically isotropic become anisotropic and display optical characteristics similar to crystals when they are stressed. This effect normally persists while the loads are maintained but vanishes when they are removed. This phenomenon is known as temporary or artificial double refraction. It is this physical characteristic of these materials on which the science of photoelasticity is based. The equipment of photoelasticity and test procedure are discussed in detail in a separate lesson.

7. **The point-by-point methods**

The extensional strain around a given point may be

determined by means of extensometers or strain gauges. These instruments measure the relative displacement between two points, the distance between the points being the so-called gauge length. In extensometers, the input is the displacement of one point relative to another. The output will be the displacement of a dial pointer, a recorder pen, or an oscilloscope trace. The *sensitivity* is defined as the ratio between the output and input. When both output and input have the same dimensions, the ratio is usually called the *gain* or *magnification*. The *resolution* is defined as the smallest possible input required to produce an observable variation in output.

8. (a) *Mechanical extensometers*. In dial gauges, the gain is achieved by means of gears. Motion is transmitted through those gears and springs pre-load the gear train to eliminate backlash. The normal gain is about 1 000, with a resolution of the order of 25×10^{-4} mm.

9. (b) *Electrical extensometers*. These are based on the measurement of the variation of resistance, inductance or capacitance in an electric displacement gauge or transducer. In variable resistance transducer, a closely coiled resistor has the two end terminals connected to a constant voltage source. A stem moves a wiper connected to a third terminal and in contact with the coil. The resolution is of the order of 25×10^{-3} mm with sensitivities of 400 mV/mm. The simplest variable inductance transducer consists of two coils with two inductors. The relative impedance of the two coils is measured by means of a movable core, the change in inductance being proportional to the core displacement.

10. (c) *Variable capacitance transducer*. Capacitance

transducers offer the advantage over the other types of their mechanical simplicity. The circuitry is on the other hand considerably more complex due to their high impedance. The sensitivity of these transducers is very high and the resolution of commercial equipment is of the order of 25×10^{-8} mm.

11. (d) *Variable resistance strain gauges*. The electrical resistance of a wire increases when the wire is stretched. The ratio between the percent change in resistance and the corresponding percent increase in length is called the *gauge factor* κ. For the metals in common use, κ varies between 0.5 and 5. Semiconductor gauges of silicon or germanium have gauge factors as high as 150.

12. A resistance strain gauge consists of a conductor, bonded to a carrier that is fixed on to the structure. The carrier may be in the form of a foil, a sheath or a frame and it may be cemented or welded to the structure. If the directions of principal axes of strain are known, the strains can be determined from two gauges positioned along these two mutually perpendicular directions. When the principal axes are not known, it is necessary to use a rosette of three gauges.

New Words and Expressions

artificial [ˌɑːtiˈfiʃəl] *adj*. 人造的,假的
backlash [ˈbæklæʃ] *n*. 反斜线(\),后座,后冲
bond [bɔnd] *n*. 结合(物),粘结(剂),债券,合同; *v*. 结合
capacitance [kəˈpæsitəns] *n*. 容量,电容
carrier [ˈkæriə] *n*. 运送者,邮递员,搬运器;[电]载波(信号)
circuitry [ˈsəːkitri] *n*. 电路,线路
coincide [ˌkəuinˈsaid] *vi*. 一致,符合

creep [kri:p] *vi.* 爬,蔓延;蠕变
crystalline ['kristəlain] *adj.* 水晶的,结晶(体)的
dial ['daiəl] *n.* 刻度盘,钟面,转盘;*v.* 拨
extensometer [ˌeksten'sɔmitə] *n.* [机]伸长计,变形测定器
foil [fɔil] *n.* 箔,金属薄片
gain [gein] *n.* 利润,收获,增益;*v.* 得到,增进
gauge [geɪdʒ] *n.* 标准尺,规格,量规,量表;*v.* 测量
germanium [dʒɔː'meiniəm] *n.* 锗
grid [grid] *n.* 格子,栅格
impedance [im'piːdəns] *n.* [电]阻抗,全电阻,[物]阻抗
inductance [in'dʌktəns] *n.* 感应系数,自感应
inscribe [in'skraib] *v.* 刻;雕;记下
interference [ˌintə'fiərəns] *n.* 冲突,干涉
interferometer [ˌintəriə'rɔmitə] *n.* 干涉计
lacquer ['lækə] *n.* 漆,漆器;*vt.* 用漆涂于…
laser ['leizə] *n.* 激光
magnification [ˌmægnifi'keiʃən] *n.* 扩大,放大倍率
monochromatic ['mɔnəukrəu'mætik] *adj.* [物]单色的,单频的
obscure [əb'skjuə] *adj.* 暗的,朦胧的,模糊的;*vt.* 使暗,使不明显
oscilloscope [ɔ'siləskəup] *n.* [物]示波器
persist [pə(ː)'sist] *vi.* 坚持,持续
photoelasticity [ˌfəutəuilæs'tisiti] *n.* 光测弹性学
pitch [pitʃ] *n.* 程度,间距,节距,斜度,投掷;*vt.* 投,掷,定位于
pointer ['pɔintə] *n.* 指示器,指针
qualitative ['kwɔlitətiv] *adj.* 性质上的,定性的
reflect [ri'flekt] *v.* 反射,反映,表现
refraction [ri'frækʃən] *n.* 折光,折射
resolution [ˌrezə'ljuːʃən] *n.* 坚定,决心;清晰度,辨析力
rosette [rəu'zet] *n.* 玫瑰形饰物,应变片花

semiconductor ['semikən'dʌktə] n. [物]半导体
sensitivity ['sensi'tiviti] n. 敏感,灵敏(度),灵敏性
sheath [ʃi:θ] n. 鞘,护套,外壳
silicon ['silikən] n. [化]硅,硅元素
slit [slit] vt. 切开,撕裂;n. 裂缝,狭长切口
stem [stem] n. 杆,柄轴,茎干,词干
trace [treis] n. 痕迹,踪迹,微量;vt. 描绘,映描,画轮廓,追踪
transducer [trænz'dju:sə] n. 传感器,变频器,变换器
transparent [træns'pɛərənt] adj. 透明的,显然的,明晰的
wiper ['waipə] n. 滑动片,滑臂;擦拭者,手帕

Lesson 36

Photoelasticity

1. When the light is such that all oscillations take place on one plane, it is said to be plane polarized. It can then be described as a standing wave similar to the ripples emanating from a source of disturbance in a pond. When the instantaneous deflection of all points remains constant and the oscillation is such that all points are constrained to move along circles perpendicular to the direction of the ray, the light is said to be circularly polarized.

2. The photoelastic bench shown in Fig. 1 consists of an instrument for the production and detection of polarized light

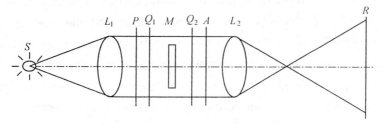

Fig. 1 Basic optical system of the polariscope

called the polariscope and a loading rig. The polariscope includes a polarizer, two quarter-wave plates, an analyzer and auxiliary optical lenses. An approximate point source S is placed at the focus of a collimating lens L_1 so that a beam of more or less parallel rays passes through the polarizer P, the first quarter-wave plate Q_1, model M, the second quarter-wave Q_1 and the analyzer A. The light emerging from the analyzer is projected by the second field lens L_2 to form an image of the model on the screen R.

3. When the polariscope does not include quarter-wave plates, the light is plane polarized by the polarizer. If the analyzer is positioned in such a way that the plane of polarization of the light emerging from the polarizer is perpendicular to the polarization plane of the analyzer, no light will be transmitted through the analyzer. Polarizer and analyzer are then said to be crossed. When the polarization planes coincide, the light is transmitted through both analyzer and polarizer which are then said to be parallel. When quarter-wave plates are added, the light becomes circularly polarized. The quarter-wave plates are always used with their optical axes at $45°$ to those of the polarizer and analyzer and they are mutually crossed.

4. When a ray of light is incident on certain crystals it is split into two components. The refractive index and the velocity of transmission are different for the two rays. Other materials such as glass, epoxy and polyester resins show this double refraction or birefringence when they are stressed. This is the property used in the photoelastic method to measure the stresses in a model.

5. A birefringent model stressed under a biaxial stress field defined by the principal stresses σ_1 and σ_2, splits the polarized ray, into two components oscillating in the directions of the principal stresses. If analyzer and polarizer are crossed, the light ray emerging from the analyzer will be

$$y = \frac{1}{2} a \{\sin \omega t - \sin \omega (t - \Delta t)\} \sin 2\beta \qquad (1)$$

where β is the angle between the plane of polarization and the σ_1-direction, a is the amplitude, and ω is the angular frequency. The condition for extinction of the emerging light is either $\beta = 0$ or $\Delta t = (2N\pi/\omega)$, where $N = 0, 1, 2, \ldots$.

6. The conditions $\beta = 0$ and $\Delta t = 0$ are independent of the wavelength. The condition $\Delta t = 2\pi/\omega, 4\pi/\omega$, etc., depends on the wavelength. When monochromatic light is used, the dark lines produced when this condition is satisfied are called fringes. With white light, the condition is only satisfied by one of the constituent colors, so that the remaining colors will give a colored line called a monochromatic.

7. The dark lines produced when the condition $\beta = 0$ is satisfied are called the isoclinics. They are the loci of all points where the principal stress directions coincide with the axes of the polarizer and the analyzer. The condition for extinction of light in the circular polariscope is $\Delta t = 2N\pi/\omega$ for the crossed polarizer-analyzer system.

8. It has been mentioned that when a plastic is stressed it becomes birefringent. Maxwell found that the difference between the refraction indices of the two refracted rays is proportional to the difference between the principal stresses. Therefore, fringes or isochromatics appear when

$$\sigma_1 - \sigma_2 = (N/h)(\lambda/c) \tag{2}$$

where h is the thickness of the model. The term (λ/c) is called the material fringe constant.

9. At an unloaded boundary, one of the two principal stresses is zero. The fringe order therefore gives a direct indication of the magnitude of the stress at a free boundary. At a loaded boundary it is difficult to determine the fringe order because of contact

stresses. However, it is possible to find both σ_1 and σ_2 if the magnitude and direction of the load are known.

10. Inside the model, the principal stresses can be separated by using one of several methods for the determination of ($\sigma_1 + \sigma_2$). For example, the sum $\sigma_1 + \sigma_2$ obeys Laplace's equation at the interior of the model, whilst at the boundary $\sigma_1 + \sigma_2$ is known. The Laplace's equation with known boundary conditions may finally be solved with an electronic computer.

New Words and Expressions

analyzer ['ænəlaizə] *n.* 检偏振镜,分析器
auxiliary [ɔ:g'ziljəri] *adj.* 辅助的,备用的
biaxial [bai'æksiəl] *adj.* 双轴的,双向的
birefringence [ˌbairi'frindʒins] *n.* 双折射
birefringent ['bairi'frindʒənt] *adj.* 双折射的
collimate ['kɔlimeit] *vt.* 校准,使成平行
deflection [di'flekʃən] *n.* 偏,偏向,挠度
detection [di'tekʃən] *n.* 探测,发现
disturbance [dis'tə:bəns] *n.* 扰动,扰乱
elasticity [ilæs'tisiti] *n.* 弹力,弹性,弹性力学
emanate ['eməneit] *vi.* 发出,发源
emerge [i'mə:dʒ] *vi.* 浮现,显露
epoxy [e'pɔksi] *adj.* 环氧的
extinction [iks'tiŋkʃən] *n.* 消灭,消失;[物]消光
focus ['fəukəs] *n.* 焦点;*v.* 聚焦
fringe [frindʒ] *n.* (干涉)条纹;边缘
incident ['insidənt] *adj.* 入射的,附带的;*n.* 事件
instantaneous [ˌinstən'teinjəs] *adj.* 即刻的,瞬间的
isoclinic [ˌaisəu'klinik] *adj.* 等倾线的,等倾向的

lens [lenz] n. 透镜,镜头
loci ['ləusai] 'locus' 的复数
locus ['ləukəs] n. 轨迹
monochromatic ['mɔnəukrəu'mætik] adj. 单色的,单频的
oscillation [ˌɔsi'leiʃən] n. 振动,摆动,振荡
parallel ['pærəlel] adj. 平行的; n. 平行
photo ['fəutəu] n. 照片
photo elasticity n. 光弹性(效应)
polariscope [pəu'læriskəup] n. 偏光器,偏振光镜
polarization [ˌpəulərai'zeiʃən; -riz-] n. 偏振,极化
polarize ['pəuləraiz] v. (使)偏振,(使)极化
polarizer ['pəuləraizə] n. 偏振镜
polyester ['pɔliestə] n. 聚酯
proportional [prə'pɔːʃənl] adj. 比例的,成比例的
refraction [ri'frækʃən] n. 折射
refractive [ri'fræktiv] adj. 折射的
resin ['rezin] n. 树脂
rig [rig] n. 装置,装备,(实验)台; v. 配备,装配
ripple ['ripl] n. 涟漪,波纹
separate ['sepəreit] adj. 分开的,分离的,个别的,单独的; v. 分开,隔离,分别
split [split] v. 劈开,(使)裂开,分裂,分离; n. 裂开,裂口,裂痕
standing ['stændiŋ] adj. 立着的,不动的;经常的,持续的
suppress [sə'pres] vt. 抑制,消除,隐藏

Lesson 37

Fracture of Brittle Materials

1. The eventual result of nearly any deformation experiment when carried far enough is the separation of the test sample into two or more pieces. Except for the case of rupture, where ultimate failure occurs when the cross-sectional area is reduced to zero, the ultimate failure of the sample is the result of some type of fracture. The simplest case of fracture is the brittle fracture which occurs at the end of the elastic extension range without extensive preceding plastic deformation. Inorganic glassed, glassy polymers at low temperatures, and ceramics are subject to brittle fracture.

2. The analysis of brittle fracture process can be simplified by the fact that the prior deformation is only elastic, and also by the fact that glassy materials are more uniform on a finer scale than crystalline materials. For reasonable assumptions about the nature of atomic binding forces, the theoretical tensile strength of a material, σ_T, can be related to Young's modulus, E, of the material. To within the uncertainty related to the lack of knowledge of the exact interatomic potential, the theoretical tensile strength is estimated to be

$$\sigma_T = \frac{E}{10} \text{ to } \frac{E}{20} \qquad (1)$$

For typical glasses, the tensile strength is on the order of 10^6 psi, which is much greater than the observed values of the fracture strength of commercial glasses, which fall in the range of 5×10^3 to 10^5 psi.

3. This large discrepancy was explained by the proposal of Griffith that glassy materials contained cracklike defects which act as stress raisers. Griffith argued that for the case of uniaxial tensile loading of a material containing a crack in the plane perpendicular to the tensile axis, the crack would begin to grow and cause ultimate failure at stresses below the theoretical strength.

4. Griffith's criterion says that if the rate of increase in surface energy resulting from the creation of a free surface by the extension of the crack is equal to the sum of the rate of the decrease in elastic strain energy around the crack and the rate of the work done by the applied constant loads, fracture can occur without requiring further increase in the external loads. From this development the breaking strength in tension, σ_c, can be related to the specific surface energy of the material, α, and the half-length of the preexisting cracks, c, by the expression

$$\sigma_c = \sqrt{\frac{2\alpha E}{\pi c}} \qquad (2)$$

5. In an alternative development, Orowan argued that in the absence of plastic deformation the radius of curvature at the tip of the crack must be nearly equal to the atomic radius a. If this value is assumed, one can calculate the local stress at the tip of the crack by using the theory of stress concentration factors given by $SCF \cong 2\sqrt{(c/a)}$. Then the microscopic fracture stress σ_c is the stress required to make the local stress at the crack tip equal to the

theoretical strength σ_T given in Eq. (1). This can be expressed as

$$\sigma_c \cong \frac{\sigma_T}{SCF} \cong \frac{E}{20}\sqrt{\frac{a}{c}} \qquad (3)$$

6. Using Eq. (3) and the measured fracture strengths of glasses, one may calculate the size of cracks necessary to account for the observed reduction in strength. Since breaking strengths of the order of 0.01 to 0.1 σ_T are commonly observed, the required stress concentration factors are of the order of 10 to 100. This requires that the material contain cracks with lengths on the order of 25 to 2 500 atomic distances or roughly 100 to 10 000 Å.

7. The question of whether defects of this severity can be expected to exist in glass and, if so, what is their origin, is an interesting one to consider here. This question is not fully answered but certain aspects of it are generally accepted. Most severe cracks in commercial glass seem to result from mechanical damage of the surface. Such damage can occur when the glass touches other hard objects. Evidence of the association of the strength-impairing defects with the surface is obtained from the fact that etching the surface of glass with hydrofluoric acid increases the strength markedly. The etch, which removes or blunts the surface cracks, can increase the strength by as much as an order of magnitude.

8. The observed strengths of etched glasses are still well below the theoretical strength. Therefore, other defects which cannot be removed by etching must exist. The nature of these defects is not fully understood. However, it has been shown that glass contains a fine cellular structure with dimensions on the order of 30 to 300 Å. The boundaries of these cells are believed to

be the origin of the defects which determine the ultimate strength of carefully prepared glass.

9. Fracture of brittle materials depends very sensitively on the volume of the material at a given stress level. This is caused by the fact that the probability of finding cracks of a given length increases with an increase in the size of the specimen. Because of this size effect, the tensile fracture stress of a uniformly loaded tensile specimen is less than the maximum tensile stress at fracture of a three-point bending test specimen, since in the bending specimen only a small portion of the material experiences stress nearly equal to the maximum stress at the surface. For this reason the tensile stress at fracture of brittle materials is sensitive to the shape of the specimen and the stress distribution. It should also be mentioned that the fracture of brittle materials is sometimes better correlated with the maximum tensile strain than with maximum tensile stress.

New Words and Expressions

acid ['æsid] n. 酸
bind [baind] v. 绑,镶边,装订,约束,使结合
blunt [blʌnt] adj. 钝的,迟钝的; vt. 弄钝,使钝; vi. 变钝
brittle ['britl] adj. 脆性的,易碎的
cell [sel] n. 单元,细胞
cellular ['seljulə] adj. 细胞的
concentration [ˌkɔnsen'treiʃən] n. 集中;浓缩,浓度;专心
correlate ['kɔrileit] vt. 使相互关联; vi. 和…相关
crystalline ['kristəlain] adj. 晶体的,结晶性的
curvature ['kə:vətʃə] n. 弯曲,曲率
damage ['dæmidʒ] n. 损伤,损害,伤害

defect [di'fekt] n. 缺陷,缺点
deformation [ˌdi:fɔ:'meiʃən] n. 变形,形变,畸变
discrepancy [dis'krepənsi] n. 不符合,差异
etch [etʃ] v. 蚀刻,腐蚀
expression [iks'preʃən] n. 表达,表达式
failure ['feiljə] n. 破坏,失败
fracture ['fræktʃə] n. 断裂,破碎
glass [glɑ:s] vi. 成玻璃状;n. 玻璃
glassy ['glɑ:si] adj. 玻璃质的,玻璃状的
hydrofluoric ['haidrəflu(:)'ɔrik] adj. 氟化氢的
impair [im'pɛə] vt. 减少,削弱;损害,伤害
inorganic [ˌinɔ:'gænik] adj. 无机的,非生物的
interatomic [ˌintərə'tɔmik] adj. 原子间的
order ['ɔ:də] n. 量级,阶数;次序;命令;定货
polymer ['pɔlimə] n. 聚合物
probability [ˌprɔbə'biliti] n. 概率,可能性
reduction [ri'dʌkʃən] n. 减少,减小
remove [ri'mu:v] v. 除去,移动
rupture ['rʌptʃə(r)] n. 破裂,断裂
separate ['sepəreit] v. (使)分离,(使)分开
severe [si'viə] adj. 严重的,严格的
severity [si'veriti] n. 严格,严重性
ultimate ['ʌltimit] adj. 终极的,极限的

Lesson 38

Linear Elastic Fracture Mechanics

1. Unlike glasses and ceramics which nearly always fail in a brittle manner, metals are generally considered to be ductile. In fact nearly all metals can be made to deform plastically at room temperature. However, some metals, particularly those with high plastic yield stresses, can be made to fracture without undergoing general yield when they contain flaws, such as notches, slots, or other severe stress concentrators. Since brittle behavior is observed for the material only when such macroscopic flaws are present, it is not proper to talk about brittle materials in these cases. It is more accurate to talk about brittle structures made from materials with limited ductility.

2. In recent years, high-strength alloys have become increasingly widely used. Because fabrication methods are often imperfect, many structures made from these materials contain cracklike defects. As a consequence of this, fracture prior to plastic yield has become an increasingly familiar mode of failure. Under these circumstances, designs based solely on resistance to plastic deformation are often inadequate when high-strength materials are used. It is, therefore, important for many applications to have a theory for metals which can either predict the breaking loads for structures containing flaws or cracks of

known geometry, or predict the maximum tolerable flaw size for a given load. The subject of relating the fracture strength of a part to the size of the flaws it contains is called fracture mechanics.

3. A starting point for developing a theory for fracture in metals would seem to be the Griffith theory, which works well for glasses and other brittle materials such as ceramics. However, this theory is meant to apply only to materials which do not undergo plastic deformation during the fracture process. Griffith made an assumption that all of the work done during fracture goes into the creation of new free surface, which does not allow for any dissipation of energy by plastic deformation. It is well concluded that even the most brittle fracture in a metal is accompanied by considerable plastic deformation in a small region at the tip of the crack. It is therefore, clear that the arguments which are used to justify the Griffith theory cannot be easily extended to apply to brittle fracture in metal structures.

4. Instead of the physical arguments on which the Griffith theory is based, an alternative argument will be used to justify the fracture criterion in the presence of a limited amount of plastic deformation. This alternative development introduces the concept of the stress intensity factor which begins with the elastic stress distribution about a sharp crack in an infinite elastic body under conditions of plane strain. The treatment given here will be concerned exclusively with cracks which are loaded by tension perpendicular to the crack. This is known as mode I loading. There are two other loading modes which are shear on the plane of the crack perpendicular to the crack front, called mode II, and shear on the plane of the crack parallel to the crack front, called mode III.

5. For the case of tensile loading, mode I, the elastic stress distribution near the crack tip is

$$\sigma_{11} = \frac{K_1}{\sqrt{2r}} \cos \frac{\theta}{2} (1 - \sin \frac{\theta}{2} \sin \frac{3\theta}{2}) \quad (1a)$$

$$\sigma_{22} = \frac{K_1}{\sqrt{2r}} \cos \frac{\theta}{2} (1 + \sin \frac{\theta}{2} \sin \frac{3\theta}{2}) \quad (1b)$$

$$\sigma_{12} = \frac{K_1}{\sqrt{2r}} \sin \frac{\theta}{2} \cos \frac{\theta}{2} \cos \frac{3\theta}{2} \quad (1c)$$

where, in the infinite body, $K_1 = \sigma_\infty \sqrt{c}$, and is called the stress intensity factor. The parameter σ_∞ is the tensile stress perpendicular to the crack applied far away from the crack, and c is the crack half-length. This solution is valid in a region where r is much less than the crack length c. The stress intensity factor is a parameter which combines information about the applied loads σ_∞ and the geometry of the body, in this case the crack length c.

6. Since the stress distribution around a sharp crack is dominated by the $1/\sqrt{r}$ crack tip singularity, the stress intensity factor completely describes the local stress distribution at the tip of a crack in an elastic body. Any combination of applied stress σ and crack length c which gives the same value of K_1 will therefore give the same stress distribution near the crack tip, even though the stresses may be different far away from the crack tip. Since the fracture process should depend only on the local stresses at or near the tip of the crack, the fracture criterion for elastic bodies should be expressible as

$$K_1 = K_{1c} \quad (2)$$

at fracture where K_{1c} is the critical stress intensity factor. The critical stress intensity factor is a material constant which in theory can be derived from the microscopic details of the fracture process.

7. The concept of the stress intensity factor can be generalized to situations other than the crack in an infinite body, such as edge cracks in a semi-infinite body and cracks in finite bodies. Since the $1/\sqrt{r}$ singularity caused by the presence of the crack tip itself dominates the stress distribution near the crack tip, the expressions for the stress distributions in other geometric situations can also be put in the form given by Eq.(1) plus additional terms which become negligible relative to the $1/\sqrt{r}$ term, when r is sufficiently small. Each geometric situation, therefore, has associated with it an expression for the stress intensity factor K_1 which is a function of the applied loads and the geometric parameters of the body. Since the stress distribution near the crack tip is uniquely determined by the stress intensity factor, the fracture criterion for the cases other than an infinite body should also be given by Eq.(2).

New Words and Expressions

argument ['ɑːgjumənt] $n.$ 争论,论点;自变量,变元;(复数的)幅角
brittle ['britl] $adj.$ 脆性的,易碎的
create [kri'eit] $v.$ 创造,引起
defect [di'fekt] $n.$ 缺陷,缺点
dissipation [ˌdisi'peiʃən] $n.$ 消耗,消散,耗散
distribution [ˌdistri'bjuːʃən] $n.$ 分布,分配
ductile ['dʌktail] $adj.$ 韧性的,易延展的
ductility [dʌk'tiliti] $n.$ 韧性,延展性
edge [edʒ] $n.$ 边缘,刀刃
fabrication [ˌfæbri'keiʃən] $n.$ 制造,建造
flaw [flɔː] $n.$ 裂纹,瑕疵,缺点

function ['fʌŋkʃən] n. 函数;功能,作用
imperfect [im'pə:fikt] adj. 不完美的,不完整的
infinite ['infinit] n. 无限的,[数]无穷大; adj. 无穷的,无限的,无数的,极大的
intensity [in'tensiti] n. 强度,强烈
linear ['liniə] adj. 线性的
mode [məud] n. 模态,样式,方式
negligible ['neglidʒəbl] adj. 可以忽略的,不足取的
notch [nɔtʃ] n. 凹槽,沟槽,刻痕
parallel ['pærəlel] adj. 平行的,相似的
parameter [pə'ræmitə] n. 参量,参数,参变量
plastic ['plæstik, plɑ:stik] adj. 塑性的,可塑的;塑料的
plastically adv. 塑性变形地
region ['ri:dʒən] n. 区域,领域
resistance [ri'zistəns] n. 抵抗,阻力;电阻,阻抗
singularity [ˌsingju'læriti] n. 奇异性;奇特;非凡
slot [slɔt] n. 缝,狭槽,细长孔
tip [tip] n. 尖端,顶;小费
tolerable ['tɔlərəbl] adj. 可容忍的,可忍受的
yield [ji:ld] n. 生产;产品;屈服,屈服(点); v. 屈服;生产,出产;产生

Lesson 39

Ductile Fracture

1. The processes of ductile fracture are extremely complex. The phenomenon depends not only on the current value of the stress and equivalent strain as does the process of plastic deformation, but on all of the details of the deformation history. Because of the complexity of the process it is not yet possible to formulate a predictive theory of ductile fracture. The discussion will therefore be limited to a qualitative description of the features which are usually observed in ductile fracture.

2. Most ductile fracture in tension appears to be associated with the development of porosity in the material caused by the growth of holes from defects. The eventual separation of the specimen results from the linking up of the holes to form the fracture surface. On the fracture surface of some materials the ridges which separate holes are very sharp, indicating that the internal strain between holes proceeded almost to rupture. The question here will be separated into a discussion of the origin of the holes and a discussion of their growth to produce the final failure.

3. In commercially pure materials and other nominally single-phase alloys, the origin of the holes most frequently appears to be impurity inclusions, most often oxides. This association is

graphically clear on the fracture surfaces of many materials where the impurity particles are found at the bottom of many dimples on the fracture surface after the failure. The origin of the hole in this case can be either a separation of the particle from the metal matrix or the cracking of the brittle particle itself.

4. In two-phase systems the origin of the holes may be the separation of the phase boundaries or cracking of the more brittle phase. In mild steel for instance, the source of the holes may be cracks in the pearlite. In some materials, especially at low temperatures, holes may result from cleavage cracks in some favorably oriented grains.

5. The initiation of the holes is not the critical step in the ductile fracture process, since the plasticity of such materials is sufficient to quickly blunt the cracks and reduce any associated stress concentration. The development of the initial holes to the larger voids which are present just prior to fracture will depend on the subsequent plastic strain and on the state of stress.

6. If the strain in the sample were to be strictly uniaxial, the holes would tend to elongate in the tension direction and become smaller in the transverse direction. This would result in long stringlike holes which would have little detrimental effect on the strength of the body.

7. However, in a tensile specimen which is deforming in a neck there are large transverse tensile stresses caused by the constraint imposed by the neck shoulders. It is the action of these stresses which tend to open up the holes into more or less spherical voids which substantially reduce the actual load-carrying area of the sample much more rapidly than the external cross-sectional area decreases.

8. Because of the fact that the transverse stresses are greatest in the center of the specimen, the ductile fracture usually begins at the center and grows outward. This is the origin of the typical cup and cone fracture. This type of fracture is composed of a central portion perpendicular to the tensile axis formed by the growth of holes in response to the transverse stresses. In a typical fine-grained ductile material, the typical fracture surface in tension is the cup and cone fracture.

9. If the entire strain to fracture is pure shear, holes cannot open in the material in the way that they do in tension. In such cases, the nature of the final failure is strongly dependent on the microstructure of the material. In a normal commercial material, inclusions and other second-phase particles create perturbations in the stress and strain which cause tension to occur locally around the particles. Cracks and holes can be formed near the particles much as they are formed in tension even when the average strain in the body is pure shear. Deformation causes the holes to elongate along the shear strain directions, and they can eventually link up to form the fracture surface.

10. However, in shear, the holes do not interact strongly with each other as they do in tension, so that much more strain is required to produce the fracture in shear. In nearly homogeneous materials, fracture is often preceded by localization of the strain on very narrow bands so that the local strain in the band becomes very large and accelerates the process of fracture.

New Words and Expressions

blunt [blʌnt] *adj*. 钝的;坦率的;*vt*. 使钝,弄钝; *vi*. 变钝
boundary ['baundəri] *n*. 边界,分界线

cleavage ['kli:vidʒ] n. 劈开,裂片,分裂
cone [kəun] n. 圆锥体,锥形
constraint [kən'streint] n. 强制,约束
detrimental [ˌdetri'mentl] adj. 有害的
dimple ['dimpl] n. 凹痕,陷窝,涟漪
ductile ['dʌktail] adj. 韧性的,易延展的
elongate ['i:lɔŋgeit] v. 延长,(使)延伸
homogeneous [ˌhɔməu'dʒi:njəs] adj. 同质的,均匀的
impurity [im'pjuəriti] n. 杂质
inclusion [in'klu:ʒən] n. 内含物,杂质,夹杂物
interact [ˌintər'ækt] v. 互相影响,交互作用
link [liŋk] n. 环,链接; v. 连结,联合
matrix ['meitriks] n. 基体,基质,母体; 矩阵
oxide ['ɔksaid] n. 氧化物
particle ['pɑ:tikl] n. 颗粒,质点,粒子
pearlite ['pə:lait] n. 珠光体(铸铁),珍珠岩
perturbation [ˌpə:tə:'beiʃən] n. 扰乱,扰动,摄动
phase [feiz] n. 相位,阶段,方面
porosity [pɔ:'rɔsiti] n. 空隙,气孔,多孔性
predictive [pri'diktiv] adj. 预测的,预言性的
proceed [prə'si:d] vi. 继续进行,开始,发出
qualitative ['kwɔlitətiv] adj. 定性的,性质上的
reduce [ri'dju:s] v. 减少,降低,缩小
ridge [ridʒ] n. 脊,背脊,山脊,屋脊; v. 起皱,成脊状延伸
rupture ['rʌptʃə(r)] n. 破裂,断裂
void [vɔid] n. 空隙,空白,空洞

Lesson 40

Fatigue in Metals

1. Fatigue fracture resulting from cyclic deformation through a few cycles of large plastic strain amplitude is familiar to most people. This phenomenon is called low-cycle fatigue, since fracture occurs after only a few strain cycles, ranging from less than ten to several hundred, depending on the amount of strain in each cycle.

2. The fact that fracture could also result from many thousand cycles of stress below the elastic limit, which is called high-cycle fatigue, was not discovered until comparatively recently, in the middle of the nineteenth century. Fatigue was first recognized as a problem in the failure of railroad car axles, and its importance has increased as mechanization has increased.

3. Because it is so important as a mode of failure, the phenomenon of fatigue has been extensively studied for more than one hundred years. Most of the early research on fatigue was confined to obtaining data for correlating the expected lifetime of a sample with the stress amplitude. The empirical relationships for fatigue lifetimes which have emerged from this research are of great engineering value. They provide the basis for the design criteria for parts subjected to cyclic loading.

4. By far the majority of experimental work on fatigue has been concerned with establishing the relationship between the stress amplitude and the number of cycles-to-failure. This work has predominantly used tension-compression or bending for loading. Since bending produces a state of stress which is locally tension or compression, these methods are equivalent. Results of such experiments are generally presented on S-N diagrams, where the stress amplitude or its logarithm is plotted as a function of the logarithm of the number of cycles-to-failure.

5. More recently, it is recognized that the total process of fatigue fracture consists of two parts. First, a crack must be formed in the material where no crack originally existed, and then it must grow until it is of sufficient size to cause the body to fail. The first portion is called crack initiation and the second is called crack propagation.

6. Much of the research on the crack initiation process has been made possible by the understanding of the mechanisms of plastic deformation which has followed the introduction of dislocation theory. Once a crack is formed, the process of interest becomes the growth of the crack. In this area, the greatest aid in understanding the phenomenon has come from the theory of fracture mechanics.

7. When a metal specimen is subjected to a strain cycle of sufficient amplitude to cause some plastic strain on each cycle, the irreversible nature of plastic deformation would lead one to expect that a gradual accumulation of damage which will lead to the formation of a crack should be occurring somewhere in the sample. The exact nature of the process by which the crack is formed is not known, but is presumed that strain concentrations

caused by grain boundaries, second-phase particles, or surface flaws must play a role. Such irregularities would cause damage accumulation to continue at some sites in the sample. For this reason, the fact that eventual failure by fracture should occur is perhaps not very surprising.

8. Under high-cycle fatigue conditions, the stress amplitude is below the yield strength of the material, so that the strain is nominally elastic. If the strain were literally purely elastic, fatigue could not result because elastic straining is, by definition, a reversible process. However, this misunderstanding is associated with the oversimplification introduced by the concept of yield strength and the assumption of purely elastic deformation below this yield strength. In fact, nearly all metals undergo a minor amount of plastic strain even at low stresses. This is called micro-strain, because at stresses well below the yield strength the magnitude of the plastic strain is small compared to the elastic strains.

9. Microscopic examination of the surfaces of samples which have been subjected to cyclic loading reveals that the micro-strain occurs inhomogeneously in the sample, with the entire strain seemingly concentrated in a relatively few isolated slip bands. Since the plastic strain amplitude in the slip bands is quite large compared to the average strain amplitude, damage accumulation leading to crack formation can continue in the slip bands at very low average plastic strain amplitudes. These slip bands form during the first few thousand cycles and remain active until after a crack is formed.

10. Once a true crack has formed in a material, the presence of the crack itself dominates the stress and strain behavior in its

vicinity. As the crack is pulled in tension, plastic flow occurs at the tip of the crack, creating a small plastic zone. The crack tip opens up and blunts out. As the stress decreases, the crack closes. At some point during the unloading or compressive portion of the cycle, the material at the crack tip begins to flow plastically in the opposite direction from the deformation in tension. As the load is reapplied, the crack advances into the region in front of the old crack tip where the material has been strained plastically from the previous cycle. Thus, the crack will move forward by a small amount on each cycle.

11. Since the stress-strain history of the crack tip is uniquely specified by the history of the stress intensity factor when the plastic deformation is limited to a suitably small region at the crack tip, it is expected that the rate of crack growth per cycle, dc/dN, should be a function of the amplitude of the change ΔK_1 of the stress intensity factor in the cycle. So the crack growth rate, dc/dN, can be expressed as

$$\frac{dc}{dN} = A\left(\frac{\Delta K_1}{\sigma_y}\right)^n \quad (1)$$

with the coefficient A and exponent n determined experimentally. The expression σ_y is the tensile yield strength of the material under investigation. In practice, the experimental correlation of crack growth rate with stress intensity factor amplitude can be regarded as very useful data in predicting fatigue fracture and service lifetimes of engineering structures.

New Words and Expressions

accumulation [əkjuːmjuˈleiʃ(e)n] $n.$ 积聚,累积
amplitude [ˈæmplitjuːd] $n.$ 幅度,振幅,波幅

axle ['æksl] *n.* 轴,车轴
band [bænd] *n.* 带子,条带;乐队;
blunt [blʌnt] *adj.* 钝的;坦率的;*vt.* 使钝,弄钝;*vi.* 变钝,减弱
concentrate ['kɔnsentreit] *v.* 集中;浓缩
confine ['kɔnfain] *n.* 界限,边界;范围,限度;*vi.* 邻接(with) *vt.* [kən'fain] 把…限制在(某范围内)
correlation [ˌkɔri'leiʃən] *n.* 相互关系,关联
cycle ['saikl] *n.* 周期,循环,轮转
damage ['dæmidʒ] *n.* 损害,伤害;*v.* 损伤,招致损害
derivative [di'rivətiv] *adj.* 引出的,派生的;*n.* 导数,微商
dislocation [ˌdislə'keiʃən] *n.* 脱臼,转位;位错
empirical [em'pirikəl] *adj.* 根据经验的,经验主义的
factor ['fæktə] *n.* 因素,因数,系数
fatigue [fə'tiːg] *n.* 疲劳
flaw [flɔː] *n.* 瑕疵,裂纹,缺点
formation [fɔː'meiʃən] *n.* 形成,构造
fracture ['fræktʃə] *n.* 断裂,破碎
inhomogeneous [ˌinhəumə'dʒiːniəs,-hɔmə-] *adj.* 非均质的,不同类的
initiation [iˌniʃi'eiʃən] *n.* 开始;发起,创始
intensity [in'tensiti] *n.* 强度,强烈
isolate ['aisəleit] *vt.* 使隔离,使绝缘
mechanism ['mekənizəm] *n.* 机械;机构;机理
nominal ['nɔminl] *adj.* 名义上的
presume [pri'zjuːm] *vt.* 假定,推测
reveal [ri'viːl] *vt.* 展现,显示,揭示,露出
reversible [ri'vɔːsəbl] *adj.* 可逆的,可反转的
slip [slip] *n.* 滑,溜;*v.* 滑动
vicinity [vi'siniti] *n.* 附近,邻近,邻域

zone [zəun] *n.* 地带,地区,区域

Lesson 41

Time-Dependent Deformation in Solids

1. In discussing the elastic deformation, it is known that elastic deformation is reversible and that it is induced by all stress components. Plastic deformation is shown to be time-independent permanent deformation, which is caused only by the distortional stress components. The term time-independent permanent deformation is used to signify the fact that a given shear stress increment in the plastic regime produced a corresponding plastic shear strain increment, regardless of the duration of loading. Implicit in this statement is the assumption that the plastic deformation occurs within a time period shorter than the usual loading period.

2. There is a third type of deformation that is irreversible, permanent, and time-dependent, called viscous deformation. Those materials which exhibit viscous behavior deform further and further as the duration of loading increases. This type of viscous behavior is exhibited by metals at high temperature and by plastics even at room temperature.

3. In a somewhat oversimplified manner, it may be stated that the genesis of viscous deformation lies in the thermal energy possessed by atoms and molecules in solids. The thermal energy of atoms is manifested in the vibration of atoms about their

equilibrium sites. Some atoms have sufficient energy to overcome the bonding energy that holds them in their equilibrium sites. If the bonding energy is denoted by E, the probability of overcoming this energy barrier is given by $\exp(-E/\kappa T)$, where κT represents the average thermal energy possessed by each atom. In the absence of any external load this probability is the same in all directions and, therefore, there is no net deformation of the solid in any particular direction.

4. In case an external shear load is applied along a given direction, the permanent switching of atomic and molecular positions along the stressed direction is favored, resulting in a gradual deformation along the loaded direction. If a tensile specimen made of polystyrene is loaded axially at room temperature, it will stretch or creep continuously at a rate determined by the probability that the energy barrier can be overcome by the thermal energy of atoms and molecules.

5. As in the plastic deformation of metals, viscous deformation is only caused by distortional stresses, and the hydrostatic component of stress primarily induces elastic volume change. The mechanical work done during viscous deformation is dissipated in the form of thermal energy. Since it can be shown that the creep rate is an exponential function of temperature, the internal dissipation of mechanical work drastically affects the overall response of a viscous material by influencing the temperature of the solid body.

6. From the foregoing discussion, it is obvious that the creep of solids depends a great deal on temperature of the solid relative to its melting point. This dependence is due to the fact that the bonding energy of atoms in a solid is directly proportional to the

melting temperature of the solid. Therefore, solids with low melting points, such as polymers and certain metals like lead, cadmium, etc., creep even at room temperature, whereas metals with high melting points, such as steel and tungsten, do not creep at noticeable rates at room temperature.

7. When a shear load is applied to a polymer, the immediate mechanism of deformation is elastic. This is followed by thermally activated creep or viscous deformation. In many structural applications, the viscous strain eventually greatly exceeds the elastic strain, so that designs can be based on the viscous component of strain exclusively. When very high loads are applied to a polymer, immediate permanent plastic deformation can result.

8. The room temperature behavior of polymers is important in design and structural applications, whereas the high temperature behavior of thermoplastics and viscous behavior of precured thermosetting plastics are of greatest interest in the materials processing field. Understanding the relationship between the chemical structure and mechanical properties can make a great deal of generalization on the mechanical behavior of polymers.

9. The preceding discussion indicates that the theory of time-dependent behavior of solids must include the effects of time. Unlike the case of elastic-plastic behavior, where stress and strain can be related without regard to rate effects, a description of a viscoelastic material must include the effects of strain rate and duration of loading.

New Words and Expressions

activate ['æktiveit] vt. 刺激,使活动; vi. 有活力

atom ['ætəm] n. 原子
barrier ['bæriə] n. 屏障,栅栏,障碍物
bond [bɔnd] v. 结合;n.结合(物),粘结(剂),债券,合同
cadmium ['kædmiəm] n. [化]镉
creep [kri:p] vi. 蠕变;爬,蔓延
dissipate ['disipeit] v. 消散,耗散,驱散,浪费(金钱或时间)
distortion [dis'tɔ:ʃən] n. 扭曲,变形,失真
distortional adj. 畸变的,扭曲的
drastic ['dræstik] adj. 激烈的,猛烈的;强有力的
drastically adv. 激烈地,彻底地
duration [djuə'reiʃən] n. 持续时间,期间
equilibrium [ˌi:kwi'libriəm] n. 平衡,均衡
function ['fʌŋkʃən] n. 功能,作用;[数]函数
generalization [ˌdʒenərəlai'zeiʃən] n. 一般化,普遍化,广义性
genesis ['dʒenisis] n. 起源,成因
hydrostatic [ˌhaidrəu'stætik] adj. 静水力学的,流体静力学的
implicit [im'plisit] adj. 暗示的,隐含的
increment ['inkrimənt] n. 增加,增量
induce [in'dju:s] vt. 导致,引起,感应
influence ['influəns] n. 影响,感化,(电磁)感应;vt. 影响,改变
irreversible [ˌiri'və:səbl,-sib-] adj. 不能撤回的,不可逆的
manifest ['mænifest] adj. 显然的,明白的; vt. 表明,证明
manifestly ['mænifestli] adv. 明白地,显然
mechanism ['mekənizəm] n. 机械装置,机构,机制,机理
melt [melt] v. (使)融化,(使)熔化
molecule ['mɔlikju:l,'məu-] n. [化]分子
polymer ['pɔlimə] n. 聚合体,聚合物
polystyrene [ˌpɔli'staiəri:n] n. 聚苯乙烯
precure ['pri:'kjuə] v. 预塑化;预硫[固化]

probability [ˌprɔbə'biliti] n. 可能性,概率
proportional [prə'pɔːʃənl] adj. 比例的,成比例的
regime [rei'ʒiːm] n. 领域,范围,政体
reversible [ri'vəːsəbl] adj. 可逆的
switch [switʃ] n. 开关,电闸,转换; vt. 转换,转变
thermoplastics [ˌθəːmə'plæstiks] n. 热塑性塑料
thermosetting [ˌθəːməu'setiŋ] adj. 热固(凝)性的
tungsten ['tʌŋstən] n. [化]钨
vibration [vai'breiʃən] n. 振动,颤动,摆动
viscoelastic [ˌviskəui'læstik] adj. [物]粘弹性的
viscous ['viskəs] adj. 粘性的,粘滞的,胶粘的
volume ['vɔljuːm;(us)-jəm] n. 卷,册;体积;大量;音量

Lesson 42

Viscous Behavior of Polymers

1. It is known that the phenomenological constitutive relationships of polymers are very complicated. Except under some special circumstances, it is difficult to generalize the behavior of polymers over a long time period, because load, temperature, and loading time affect the constitutive relationship. However, it is clear that polymers behave in a viscoelastic-plastic manner. At low temperatures and high loads, the elastic and plastic deformations dominate, whereas at high temperatures and high loads, the viscous behavior is more important.

2. One of the distinguishing characteristics of the mechanical behavior of polymers at room temperature under a moderate load is viscoelasticity. The viscoelastic nature of polymers may be

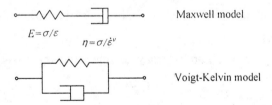

Fig. 1 Spring and dashpot models for a viscoelastic solid.

approximately modeled by spring-dashpot systems. Two of the well-known models are the Maxwell model and the Voigt-Kelvin model. As shown in Fig. 1, these models describe linear viscoelasticity, which is an approximation to real viscoelastic behavior of polymers. Certain generalizations can be made by using these models, although the past attempts to develop a constitutive relationship for real solids using a combination of many springs and dashpots have been largely unsuccessful.

3. Qualitatively, it is shown by the Maxwell model that at the instant of loading, the solid behaves elastically, and then viscous deformation occurs, since the spring deforms instantaneously and the deformation rate of the dashpot is proportional to the applied stress. In the case of the Voigt-Kelvin solid there is no instantaneous deformation, and the maximum strain is limited by the spring.

4. Although the mechanical behavior of real polymers cannot be modeled perfectly by combinations of springs and dashpots, many characteristics of real polymers can be understood from the characteristics of the simple Maxwell and Voigt-Kelvin models. Consider the constitutive relationship for the Maxwell model, the total strain ε_{ij} is the sum of elastic and viscous deformation, i.e.,

$$\varepsilon_{ij} = \varepsilon_{ij}^e + \varepsilon_{ij}^v \tag{1}$$

where ε_{ij}^e is the elastic strain, and ε_{ij}^v is the strain due to the viscous part.

5. The strains ε_{ij}^e and ε_{ij}^v may be related to the stresses by

$$\varepsilon_{11}^e = \sigma_{11}/E \tag{2}$$

$$d\varepsilon_{11}^v/dt = \sigma_{11}/\eta \tag{3}$$

Differentiating Eqs. (1) and (2), and combining them with Eq. (3), the constitutive relation for the Maxwell solid may be written as

$$\frac{d\varepsilon_{11}}{dt} = \frac{1}{E}\frac{d\sigma_{11}}{dt} + \frac{\sigma_{11}}{\eta} \qquad (4)$$

The constitutive relationship for the Voigt-Kelvin model may similarly be derived.

6. From Eq. (4) it is seen that the usual stress-strain relationship obtained by tensile testing will be very sensitively dependent on the strain rate. For a material with very large viscosity or under high loading rates, the Maxwell solid behaves as a Hookeian solid and the Voigt-Kelvin solid behaves as a rigid solid. In this respect, the behavior of polymers is more closely represented by the Maxwell model than by the Voigt-Kelvin model.

7. Of course, real polymers cannot adequately be described in terms of these simple models. By adding more springs and dashpots, one can approximate the real behavior, at least in theory. The constitutive relation for any arbitrary number of these elements may be represented as

$$\sum_{m=0}^{a} P_m \frac{d^m \sigma_{ij}'}{dt^m} = \sum_{n=0}^{b} q_n \frac{d^n \varepsilon_{ij}'}{dt^n} \qquad (5)$$

where the terms P_m and q_n are constants. Equation (5) only includes the deviator components of stress and strain. The hydrostatic compression of viscoelastic materials is elastic, and, therefore, the hydrostatic components of stress and strain can be related in terms of the bulk modulus of the material.

8. Equation (5) is a linear ordinary differential equation. A solid whose constitutive relationship can be represented by Eq. (5) is called linear viscoelastic. Note the proportionality constants P_m and q_n are independent of the magnitude of the applied stress. Therefore, in a linear viscoelastic solid under a constant stress distribution, strain is always linearly proportional to stress at any

given time. Real polymers behave in a linear viscoelastic manner over a limited range of load. Over a wider range of load, the behavior is nonlinear.

New Words and Expressions

approximately [əprɔksi'mətli] *adv*. 近似地,大约
bulk [bʌlk] *n*. 大小,体积,块,大批
characteristic [ˌkæriktə'ristik] *adj*. 特有的,典型的; *n*. 特性,特征
circumstance ['sɔːkəmstəns] *n*. 环境,详情,境况
compression [kəm'preʃ(ə)n] *n*. 压缩,浓缩,压榨
constitutive ['kɔnstitjuːtiv] *adj*. 构成的,基本的,本质的,[物]本构的
dashpot ['dæʃˌpɔt] *n*. 阻尼器,缓冲器
deviator ['diːvieitə] *n*. 偏差器,偏量
differential [ˌdifə'renʃəl] *adj*. 微分的; *n*. 微分
differentiate [ˌdifə'renʃieit] *v*. 区别,区分,求…的微分
distribution [ˌdistri'bjuːʃən] *n*. 分布,分配,区分,发行
generalization [ˌdʒenərəlai'zeiʃən] *n*. 一般化,普遍化,广义性
generalize ['dʒenərəlaiz] *vt*. 归纳,概括,推广,普及
hydrostatic [ˌhaidrəu'stætik] *adj*. 静水力学的
instantaneous [ˌinstən'teinjəs] *adj*. 瞬间的,即刻的,即时的
linear ['liniə] *adj*. 直线的,线性的
model ['mɔdl] *n*. 样式,模型; *vt*. 模仿
nonlinear ['nɔnːliniə] *adj*. 非线性的
phenomenological [fiˌnɔminə'lɔdʒikəl, fə-] *adj*. 现象学的,现象的
plastic ['plæstik, plaːstik] *adj*. 塑性的; *n*. 塑胶,塑料制品
polymer ['pɔlimə] *n*. 聚合体,聚合物
proportional [prə'pɔːʃnl] *adj*. 成比例的,相称的,均衡的
proportionality [prəˌpɔːʃə'næliti] *n*. 比例(性),均衡(性)

qualitatively ['kwɔlitətivli] adv. 质量上,定性的
quality ['kwɔliti] n. 质量,品质,性质
rate [reit] n. 比率,速率,等级,价格
sensitive ['sensitiv] adj. 敏感的,灵敏的
spring [spriŋ] n. 春天,泉,弹簧; v. 跳,跃出
viscoelastic [ˌviskəui'læstik] adj. [物]粘弹性的
viscosity [vis'kɔsiti] n. 粘质,粘性
viscous ['viskəs] adj. 粘性的,粘滞的,胶粘的

Lesson 43

Creep in Metals

1. The time-independent theory of plastic deformation assumes that the stress required to cause plastic deformation is independent of the rate of deformation. The justification for this approximation is that the tensile stress-strain curves measured at room temperature are changed by only a few percent when the strain rate is changed by an order of magnitude. Under static loading conditions, the strain rate is of no engineering significance when a static stress is applied.

2. This type of behavior is typical of a metal at temperatures below about one-third of its melting point on an absolute temperature scale. As the temperature is raised above one-third of the melting temperature, these approximations become increasingly inaccurate. In general the effects of increasing the temperature on the mechanical properties of metals are to decrease both the yield strength and the modulus, and to increase the strain rate dependence of the stress-strain curves.

3. Definition of a general yield strength becomes increasingly difficult, and standard strain rates must be used in short-time tensile tests to ensure reproducibility of the results. In terms of behavior under static loading, it is found that loads well below the short-time yield strength will cause straining at appreciable rates,

and that maintaining these loads for long periods of time may eventually cause fracture. This phenomenon of slow straining at constant stress at elevated temperature is called creep.

4. To conduct a typical high-temperature creep experiment, a constant load is applied to the specimen and the strain is measured as a function of time. A small amount of elastic strain accompanies the application of the load. This elastic component of strain is present as long as the load is maintained and is recoverable by unloading at any stage of the experiment. As the time under load increases, the strain in the specimen increases continuously. This additional strain is permanent.

5. The creep process is traditionally divided into three stages. The first stage, which is called transient or primary creep, is characterized by a relatively high strain rate which decreases with time. The strain rate eventually reaches a minimum value which may remain constant for some period of time. This stage is called steady-state or secondary creep. At some point, another transition occurs and the creep rate again accelerates. This final stage which is terminated by the fracture of the sample is called tertiary creep. The relative durations of the three stages depend on the temperature, stress, and prior history of the sample.

6. There are a number of strain-producing processes which can occur only at elevated temperature and contribute to creep. The mechanism which limits the rate of creep is probably diffusion-controlled climb of dislocations. However, thermally activated glide of dislocations, grain boundary sliding, and direct mass transfer by diffusion may also contribute to the creep process. At relatively low temperatures close to one-third of the melting temperature, diffusion rates are small and direct thermal

activation of dislocations probably accounts for most of the creep strain. At very high temperatures and low stresses, where dislocation processes are slow, the rate of diffusion may become sufficiently large that direct mass transport by diffusion becomes the rate controlling process.

7. Since many applications require the use of metals at temperatures where creep is significant, a theory is needed to allow the use of experimental data to predict the service behavior of engineering structures. The ideas to be presented will first be illustrated by the simple case of uniaxial stress. The results will then be generalized to more complex states of stress.

8. Primary creep usually obeys the functional relation

$$\varepsilon_{11} = \beta t^{1/3} \tag{1}$$

where t is the time of loading, and β is a function of the stress, temperature, and prior strain history. Because of this prior history dependence, consistent data for the evaluation of β and its dependence on stress and temperature are rarely available. However, for engineering purposes involving materials with a uniform prior history, the necessary information can be obtained from a series of short-term experiments.

9. During steady-state creep, the creep rate should be independent of the strain and relatively insensitive to prior history. Since the above discussion indicates that the rate limiting process in creep is thermally activated, a typical Arrhenius type relationship is expected, i.e.,

$$\dot{\varepsilon}_{11} = A\sigma_{11}^m \exp\left[-\frac{H(\sigma_{11})}{\kappa T}\right] \tag{2}$$

where the term σ_{11}^m is inserted to account for the effects of stress on the steady-state dislocation structure, and the stress dependence of the activation energy H reflects the fact that thermal activation is assisted by the applied stress.

10. Over the range of interest, A and m can be considered to be constant and H to be a function of stress only. In Eq.(2), κ is Boltzmann's constant. Complete description of the creep process, therefore, requires determination of the two conatants, A and m, and the stress-dependent function H from experimental data.

New Words and Expressions

accelerate [æk'seləreit] $v.$ 加速,促进
accompany [ə'kʌmpəni] $vt.$ 陪伴,伴随,伴奏
activate ['æktiveit] $vt.$ 刺激,使活动; $vi.$ 有活力
activation [ˌækti'veiʃən] $n.$ 活化,激活,[化]活化作用
approximation [əˌprɔksi'meiʃən] $n.$ 接近,走近,[数]近似值
assist [ə'sist] $v.$ 援助,帮助
characterize ['kæriktəraiz] $vt.$ 表现…的特色,刻画的…性格
climb [klaim] $v.$ 攀登,爬; $n.$ 攀登,爬
creep [kri:p] $vi.$ 蠕变,蠕动,爬,蔓延
diffusion [di'fju:ʒən] $n.$ 扩散,传播,漫射
dislocation [ˌdislə'keiʃən] $n.$ 位错;断层,脱臼
fracture ['fræktʃə] $n.$ 破裂,断裂,骨折; $v.$ (使)破碎,(使)破裂
generalize ['dʒenərəlaiz] $vt.$ 归纳,概括,推广,普及
glide [glaid] $v.$ 滑行,滑翔; $n.$ 滑行,滑翔,滑移,滑音
inaccurate [in'ækjurit] $adj.$ 不准确的,错误的
insensitive [in'sensitiv] $adj.$ 感觉迟钝的,低灵敏度的
justification [dʒʌstifi'keiʃ(ə)n] $n.$ 认为有理,认为正当,理由,调整,辩护,释罪
melt [melt] $v.$ (使)融化,(使)熔化,使软化
modulus ['mɔdjuləs] $n.$ 系数,模量,模数

permanent ['pə:mənənt] *adj.* 永久的,持久的
phenomenon [fi'nɔminən] *n.* 现象
recoverable [ri'kʌvərəbl] *adj.* 可再现的,可重获的
reflect [ri'flekt] *v.* 反射,反映,表现,反省
reproducibility [riprə‚dju:sə'biliti] *n.* 重复能力,再现性
terminate ['tə:mineit] *v.* 停止,结束,终止
tertiary ['tə:ʃəri] *adj.* 第三的,第三位的
yield [ji:ld] *n.* 屈服; *v.* 产出,生产; *vi.* (~ to) 屈服于,屈从

Lesson 44

Friction and Wear of Materials

1. In general, an understanding of bulk behavior is important in analyzing the deformation of materials under a given set of external loads and in determining the fracture load of structural parts. Attention will now shift to another aspect of the mechanical behavior of materials-the study of surface phenomena. In particular, friction, wear, adhesion, and lubrication of material surfaces will be discussed.

2. In choosing engineering materials for such applications as bearings, cams, sliding surfaces, shafts, turbine blades, helicopter rotors, crude oil pipelines, fountain pen points, and automobile tires, the surface properties of materials must be considered in conjunction with the bulk properties. For some applications, the surface characteristics may be the decisive factor in material selection.

3. From experience with sliding surfaces, it is known that it takes a nonzero force to slide one solid surface over another surface. In other words, work is done between sliding surfaces. All this work is somehow consumed at the interface, while the bulk of the solid remains essentially unchanged. The question then is how the work is consumed at the surface. There are three major modes of energy consumption operating between the sliding

surfaces. If any plastic and viscous deformations are involved at the interface, a part of the work done is transformed into thermal energy which raises the interface temperature. In many applications this mode of energy consumption is most important. The work done may also be consumed in creating new surfaces or interfaces. This occurs when wear particles and internal voids are generated and when the interface deforms. Finally, it may be stored in the form of residual elastic strain energy at the surface.

4. The first step in understanding the friction and wear of metals is to consider the topography of solid surfaces. This aspect has been experimentally investigated using optical instruments, such as metallographs and electron microscopes, and mechanical tracing instruments, such as surface profilometers. According to these investigations, the surface of a metal is not smooth, but rather is made up of many asperities (tiny peaks). Therefore, when two metal surfaces are in contact, the real area of contact is much smaller than the apparent area of contact. The interaction of these asperities with adjoining surfaces governs the friction and wear behavior of solids.

5. It has been found that, under normal load, as the highest asperities are flattened, in some cases the remainder of the surface will rise. Depending on the shape of the surface profile, the number of asperities in contact and the projected area of contact change, so that the normal load L is equal to the product of the real area of contact, A, times the normal stress at each asperity.

6. It is now generally well recognized that sliding friction between solids is primarily controlled by the following two main mechanisms: the degree and quality of adhesion between the two sliding surfaces, and the plowing of the soft surface layers by hard

asperities. The degree and quality of adhesion are influenced by the surface energy and the surrounding environment. The adhesion theory of friction assumes that complete adhesion exists between the contact surfaces of asperities. Although the 'plowing' mechanism may be more important than the adhesion mechanism in many sliding situations, there is as yet no theoretical model for 'plowing'.

7. Consider a slider block lying on a flat surface subjected to both normal load L and tangential load F. When the tangential force F, which is less than a critical value $F_{\max}$, is applied to the block, it will not move. The static coefficient of friction is defined as the minimum tangential force required to initiate the tangential motion, $F_{\min}$, divided by the normal load L acting on the interface, i.e.,

$$\mu = F_{\min}/L \tag{1}$$

The coefficient μ is found to be independent of the apparent area of contact, the normal load, and the duration of loading.

8. It is known that the real area of contact is smaller than the apparent area of contact. The adhesion theory of friction states that the junctions formed at the real area of contact adhere to each other, and that for sliding to occur these junctions must be sheared. When two surfaces slide over each other, the friction force must be equal to the product of the shear stress required to deform these junctions plastically and the area of these junction, i.e.,

$$F = \tau \cdot A \tag{2}$$

where τ is the shear strength of the junctions. When the applied load is so small that the asperities cannot penetrate through the contaminant layer on the surface, the magnitude of τ will be dictated by the shear strength of the contaminants. As the applied normal load is increased, the asperities can penetrate through the contaminants and junctions may be formed between the base metals.

9. When metal-to-metal contact is established at these junctions, the critical shear strength τ may be assumed to be about equal to the strength to deform the weaker metal plastically. τ is normally assumed to be equal to the bulk shear strength of the weaker metal.

New Words and Expressions

adhere [əd'hiə] v. 粘附,粘固
adhesion [əd'hi:ʒən] n. 附着力,粘附力
adjoin [ə'dʒɔin] vt. 与…相连(相接); vi. 连接,邻接,邻近
asperity [æs'periti] n. 粗糙(度),凹凸,突起物
bearing ['bɛəriŋ] n. 轴承
blade [bleid] n. 叶片
bulk [bʌlk] n. 大块,体积,大小
cam [kæm] n. 凸轮
coefficient [kəui'fiʃənt] n. 系数
contaminant [kən'tæminənt] n. 污染,污物,杂质
crude [kru:d] adj. 天然的,粗糙的
friction ['frikʃən] n. 摩擦
helicopter ['helikɔptə] n. 直升机
initiate [i'niʃieit] vt. 开始,发动,发起; vi. 开始
lubrication [ˌlu:bri'keiʃən] n. 润滑
mechanism ['mekənizəm] n. 机构,结构,机理
metallograph [mi'tæləgrɑ:f] n. (金属表面)显微照相
optical ['ɔptikəl] adj. 光学的

peak [piːk] n. 尖峰,顶点; adj. 最大值的
penetrate ['penitreit] vt. 穿透,渗透;看穿,洞察; vi. 刺入,弥漫,看穿
pipeline ['paipˌlain] n. 管道
plow [plau] v. 犁,耕,费力穿过; n. 犁
profile ['prəufail] n. 侧面,轮廓
profilometer [ˌprəufi'lɔmitə] n. [机]轮廓曲线仪,表面光度仪,表面(粗糙度)测定仪
residual [ri'zidjuəl] adj. 剩余的,残留的
rotor ['rəutə] n. 转子,转动体
shaft [ʃɑːft] n. 轴
shift [ʃift] n. 移动,移位;轮班; vt. 替换,转移,改变,移转; vi. 转换,移动,转变
slide [slaid] v. (使)滑动,(使)滑行; n. 滑,滑动,幻灯片
tangential [tæn'dʒenʃ(ə)l] adj. 切线的,相切的
topography [tə'pɔgrəfi] n. 地形学,形貌,构形
turbine ['təːbin,-bain] n. 涡轮机
viscous ['viskəs] adj. 粘性的,粘滞的
void [vɔid] n. 空隙,空洞
wear [wiə] n. 磨损,损耗,耐磨性;穿破; v. 磨损;穿;戴着

Lesson 45

Basic Equations of Fluid Mechanics

1. A fluid is a substance, such as gas or liquid, that will deform continuously under the action of applied surface stresses. Different fluids show different relations between stress and the rate of deformation. Depending on the nature of relation followed between stress and rate of deformation, fluids can be classified into Newtonian and non-Newtonian fluids.

2. A Newtonian fluid is one in which the shear stress is directly proportional to the rate of deformation starting with zero stress and zero deformation. The constant of proportionality is defined as μ, the absolute or dynamic viscosity. Common examples of Newtonian fluids are air and water.

3. A non-Newtonian fluid is one which has a variable proportionality between stress and rate of deformation. Common examples of non-Newtonian fluids are some of the plastics, colloidal suspensions and emulsions.

4. A flow may be termed as inviscid or viscous depending on the importance of consideration of viscosity of the fluid in the analysis. An inviscid flow is a frictionless flow characterized by zero viscosity. A viscous flow is one in which the fluid is assumed to have nonzero viscosity.

5. Although no real fluid is inviscid, there are several flow

situations in which the effect of viscosity of the fluid can be neglected. For example, in the analysis of a flow over a body surface, the viscosity effects are considered in a thin region close to the flow boundary, which is known as boundary layer, while the viscosity effect is neglected in the rest of the flow.

6. Fluids can also be divided into two categories depending on the property of compressibility as compressible and incompressible fluids. Usually liquids are treated as incompressible while gases and vapors are assumed to be compressible.

7. In most engineering problems, the fluids can be considered for all practical purposes incompressible and inviscid. With these hypotheses the fluids will only withstand pressure forces and will react without changing volume. Consider a particle located in two-dimensional space and take the actual coordinates x, y and the time t as independent variables, we will refer the particle to a special system, called an Eulerian reference frame. Any quantity such as pressure, velocity etc. are functions of position and time. In general

$$f = f(x, y, t) \tag{1}$$

where f denotes the variable associated with the point (x, y) at time t.

8. During the time increment, the material point moves from x to $x + \Delta x$, y to $y + \Delta y$ and the variable f changes to $f + \Delta f$. Assuming f to be a continuous function we can write

$$\frac{df}{dt} = \lim_{\Delta t \to 0}(\frac{\partial f}{\partial x}\frac{\Delta x}{\Delta t} + \frac{\partial f}{\partial y}\frac{\Delta y}{\Delta t} + \frac{\partial f}{\partial t}) = u\frac{\partial f}{\partial x} + v\frac{\partial f}{\partial y} + \frac{\partial f}{\partial t} \tag{2}$$

Since we are now actually following the material point or particle, the term "material" derivative is used for $D( )/Dt$. The first two terms in Eq.(2) are the convective terms and the last the "local" time derivative.

9. The two-dimensional state of stress for a fluid can be defined as for a solid, in terms of σ_x, σ_y, τ stress components at any point and time. If the fluid is incompressible its density ρ will remain constant and the equilibrium equations can be written as,

$$\frac{\partial \sigma_x}{\partial x} + \frac{\partial \tau}{\partial y} + \rho b_x = \rho \frac{\mathrm{d}u}{\mathrm{d}t}; \qquad \frac{\partial \tau}{\partial x} + \frac{\partial \sigma_y}{\partial y} + \rho b_y = \rho \frac{\mathrm{d}v}{\mathrm{d}t} \qquad (3)$$

10. The boundary regions of a fluid can be classified into two zones. The zone S_v represents the surface area on which the velocities are prescribed. If S_v is a physical boundary such as a wall, the velocity components are $v_n = 0$ and $v_s \neq 0$. Symmetry and inflow velocity constraints are also included in S_v.

11. S_ρ is defined as the surface zone on which prescribed boundary forces are acting, for instance normal and tangential forces acting on the boundary of the fluid. If the fluid is inviscid, tangential forces cannot be imposed and we can only apply normal pressures.

12. Fluids which are inviscid and incompressible are called perfect fluids and obey mathematical relationships which greatly simplify the problem. Let us deduce the incompressibility relation by considering an element of fluid at time t. In order to have continuity it is necessary that the amount of fluid entering the differential volume be equal to the amount leaving it. This flow-in, flow-out relationship implies that

$$\frac{\partial u}{\partial x} + \frac{\partial v}{\partial y} = 0 \qquad (4)$$

Eq. (4) is called the continuity or incompressibility condition.

13. Let us consider what happens when the fluid is inviscid, i. e., the viscosity $\mu = 0$. We cannot apply shear forces to such a

fluid, which physically means that the fluid particle cannot equilibrate any shear forces. Hence we cannot produce rotation in an inviscid fluid particle. This condition is called the irrotationality condition and can be written mathematically as

$$\omega = \frac{1}{2}(\frac{\partial v}{\partial x} - \frac{\partial u}{\partial y}) = 0 \qquad (5)$$

where ω is the angular velocity about the z axis.

14. For graphical representation of fluid motion, it is convenient to introduce the concept of streamline. A line drawn in the fluid so that its tangent at each point is in the direction of the fluid velocity at that point is called a streamline. Thus the streamlines represent the direction of motion at each point along the line at a given instant.

15. The fluid loss between two streamlines at a differential distance is

$$d\psi = u dy - v dx = \frac{\partial \psi}{\partial y} dy + \frac{\partial \psi}{\partial x} dx \qquad (6)$$

Thus, $u = \partial \psi / \partial y$, $v = - \partial \psi / \partial x$, which define the stream function ψ for a two-dimensional incompressible flow. Using the stream function, we obtain

$$\frac{\partial^2 \psi}{\partial x^2} + \frac{\partial^2 \psi}{\partial y^2} = 0 \qquad (7)$$

It is shown that the above Laplace's equation can be solved for the solution of a two-dimensional irrotational and incompressible flow.

New Words and Expressions

angular ['æŋgjulə] *adj*. 角的,角度的,有角的
colloidal [kə'lɔidl] *adj*. 胶状的,胶质的
compressibility [kəmˌpresi'biliti] *n*. 可压缩性
constraint [kən'streint] *n*. 约束,强制

convective [kən'vektiv] *adj.* 对流的,传送性的
derivative [di'rivətiv] *adj.* 派生的,导出的; *n.* 派生物,导数,微商
dynamic [dai'næmik] *adj.* 动态的,动力的
emulsion [i'mʌlʃən] *n.* 乳状液,乳剂
equilibrate [ˌiːkwi'laibreit] *v.* 与…平衡
equilibrium [ˌiːkwi'libriəm] *n.* 平衡
fluid ['fluː(ː)id] *n.* 流体,液体
friction ['frikʃən] *n.* 摩擦
hypothesis [hai'pɔθisis] *n.* 假设
increment ['inkrimənt] *n.* 增值,增量
inviscid [in'visid] *adj.* 非粘滞性的,无韧性的,不能展延的
layer ['leiə] *n.* 层
normal ['nɔːməl] *n.* 正规,常态,[数学]法线; *adj.* 正常的,正规的,标准的,法向的
rotation [rəu'teiʃən] *n.* 旋转,轮流
streamline ['striːmlain] *n.* 流线,流线型
suspension [səs'penʃən] *n.* 悬,悬浮,挂,停止
symmetry ['simitri] *n.* 对称,匀称
tangential [tæn'dʒenʃ(ə)l] *adj.* 切线的,切向的
vapor ['veipə] *n.* 汽,蒸气
variable ['vɛəriəbl] *n.* 变量; *adj.* 可变的
viscosity [vis'kɔsiti] *n.* 粘性
viscous ['viskəs] *adj.* 粘性的

Lesson 46

Civil Engineering

1. Civil engineering is claimed to be the art of directing the great sources of power in nature for the use and convenience of man. The part played by civil engineers in pioneering work and in developing wide areas of the world has been and continues to be enormous. Civil engineers must make use of many different branches of knowledge including mathematics, theory of structures, hydraulics, soil mechanics, surveying, hydrology, geology and economics.

2. Civil engineering was not distinguished from other branches of engineering until 200 years ago. Most early engineers were engaged in the construction of fortifications and were responsible for building the roads and bridges required for the movement of troops and supplies. The Roman armies of occupation in Europe were served by brilliant engineers but after the collapse of the Roman empire there was little progress in communications until the beginning of the Industrial Revolution, the invention of the steam engine and the realization of the potentialities in the use of iron. Roads, canals, railways, ports, harbors and bridges were then built by engineers who adopted the prefix 'civil' to distinguish them from the military engineers and to emphasize the value of their work to the community.

3. Let us look briefly at some of the problems of building bridges and dams. Wood, brick and stone were generally used in constructing bridges until the nineteenth century. Many stone bridges in the United Kingdom are several hundred years old. The first iron bridge was completed in 1779. Iron was commonly used for bridge construction for more than one hundred years. Iron has been replaced by steel, which is stronger, and permits lighter members to be used. Bridges are now made of steel or of reinforced concrete, or of steel and reinforced concrete combined, or even of aluminium alloy.

4. Many modern bridges are made of concrete beams supported by concrete piers and abutments. Concrete is strong in compression, but weak in tension. Steel, which is strong in tension, is used to counteract the tensile forces in loaded beams. For abutments and piers and also beams, an arrangement of steel wires or rods is encased in concrete, to make reinforced concrete. When a beam is supported at its ends, the upper part of the beam is in compression and the lower part is in tension. When the beam is subjected to a heavy load the stresses are increased. If a beam is made of concrete it is usually strengthened or reinforced by means of steel rods in the lower part of the beam where the tensile stresses are found.

5. Suspension bridges are generally used for very long spans. A pair of cables, anchored at both ends, is supported on towers. The deck is joined to the cables by suspenders. The cables are in tension, and are usually made of many thousands of fine steel wires, which together have a greater tensile strength than ordinary steel. The deck is generally made of reinforced concrete or steel. The design of suspension bridges continues to be improved. In a

bridge recently built the cross-section of the deck has been streamlined to minimize the effects of cross-winds. The hollow steel boxes of which this deck is constructed require less steel than a solid deck of the same strength. The lighter deck can be supported by lighter cables and suspenders. Thus the new design economizes on the use of steel.

6. The modern dam can serve one purpose, or several purposes, including storage of water for water supply, generation of hydro-electric power, irrigation of agricultural land and the regulation of rivers to prevent disastrous floods. A dam consists basically of three parts:

(1) A wall of concrete or embankment of earth or rock, which prevents the passage of water.
(2) A means of releasing water stored upstream of the dam, usually by tunnel or pipeline.
(3) A means of passing flood waters through or over the dam into the river channel below it, i.e., the spillway.

7. Concrete dams are, generally speaking, feasible in steep-sided valleys or gorges where hard rock can be found on which to place the dam structure. Gravity dams in concrete are the most usual type, where water pressure on the upstream face is resisted by the mass of the dam. Such dams may be of plain construction, like a wedge in shape, the point being upwards, and in many instances are built as a number of buttresses, which can lead to economy in materials.

8. All dams need sound foundations, and the nature of the bedrock under many dams entails extensive grouting of fissures and porous zones with cement or with chemicals to prevent water passing under or round the dam. Spillways which can safely pass

floodwater are of many types, and often require the boring of large tunnels. Tunnels are also used to supply water to power stations, and may be combined with the steel penstocks which are often the only visible evidence of hydroelectric power schemes. It is vital to remember that a dam is designed to stop the passage of water and to store it. Without means of controlling and passing both normal and flood flows round or through the dam, the safety of the dam and of the people living in its shadow and further downstream could not be assured.

New Words and Expressions

abutment [ə'bʌtmənt] n. 邻接,接界,桥台
anchor ['æŋkə] n. 锚; v. 固定,栓住
bore [bɔ:] n. 孔,枪膛; v. 钻孔
buttress ['bʌtris] n. 拱壁,扶壁,支持物
canal [kə'næl] n. 沟渠,运河,水道
civil ['sivl] adj. 土木工程的,民用的
collapse [kə'læps] vi. 倒塌,崩溃; vt. 使倒塌,使崩溃;
    n. 倒塌,崩溃;断裂
counteract [ˌkauntə'rækt] vt. 抵消,中和,抵抗,抵制
dam [dæm] n. 水坝
deck [dek] n. 甲板
disastrous [di'zɑ:strəs] adj. 悲伤的,损失惨重的
distinguish [dis'tiŋgwiʃ] v. 区别,辨别
embankment [im'bæŋkmənt] n. 堤防,筑堤
enormous [i'nɔ:məs] adj. 巨大的,庞大的
entail [in'teil] vt. 使必需,使承担,需要,遗传给
fissure ['fiʃə] n. 裂缝,裂沟; v. (使)裂开,(使)分裂
flood [flʌd] n. 洪水,涨潮

fortification [ˌfɔːtifiˈkeiʃən] n. 筑城，防御工事
geology [dʒiˈɔlədʒi] n. 地质学
gorge [gɔːdʒ] n. 峡谷，凹槽
grout [graut] n. 水泥浆；v. 用薄泥浆填塞
harbor [ˈhɑːbə] n. 港，海港，港口；v. 入港停泊；隐匿
hydraulics [ˈhaiˈdrɔːliks] n. 水力学
hydrology [haiˈdrɔlədʒi] n. 水文学
penstock [ˈpenstɔk] n. 闸门，给水栓；水道，水渠
pier [piə] n. 码头，桥墩
porous [ˈpɔːrəs] adj. 多孔的
potentiality [pəˌtenʃiˈæliti] n. 潜在性；潜能，潜力
reinforce [ˌriːinˈfɔːs] v. 加强，加固，增援
soil [sɔil] n. 土壤，土地
span [spæn] n. 跨距，指距
spillway [ˈspilwei] n. 溢洪道，泄洪道
survey [sɔːˈvei] n. 测量，调查，纵览，概观；vt. 调查，测量，勘定
suspender [səˈspendə(r)] n. 悬挂者(物)，吊杆，吊裤带
suspension [səsˈpenʃən] n. 悬挂，暂停，中止
tunnel [ˈtʌnl] n. 隧道，地下道
valley [ˈvæli] n. 山谷，溪谷，凹地
wedge [wedʒ] n. 楔子，楔形物
zone [zəun] n. 地区，地带，区域

Lesson 47

The Airplanes

1. It was December, 1903, in the southeastern United States. Strong winds bent the grass near the beach, and the smell of salt air came in from the Atlantic Ocean. A small group of men were standing near a strange flying machine. One of them, whose name was Wilbur Wright, began to push the machine along a rail, while another-his brother Orville-lay on the lower wing and grasped the simple controls. Only five persons were there to see the clumsy craft rise from the ground as Wilbur ran faster and faster. After flying only 120 feet, it touched the ground again and slid to a stop. Man had flown the first successful airplane with a gasoline engine.

2. Since the days of the Wright brothers, many improvements have been made in the construction and design of airplanes. Probably the greatest improvement in air transportation has been the jet engine. Piston-engines, which drive propellers, use comparatively little fuel and are relatively efficient at low speeds and at altitudes of less than seven thousand meters. However, piston-engined airplane cannot attain speeds in excess of about eight hundred kilometers per hour. Turbo-jet engines, or 'pure' jet engines, perform most economically at high cruising speeds and at altitudes of seven thousand meters or more. Near the ground there is considerable loss of performance and fuel consumption

rises to uneconomical proportions. Turbo-prop engines, in which the turbines drive propellers, combine some of the advantages of both piston and pure jet engines. Speeds of up to seven hundred kilometers per hour at operating heights of about six thousand meters are attained economically and landing and take-off performance is good.

3. The simplest way to understand how a jet engine works is to watch air escaping from a balloon. As the air escapes, it creates a back pressure that pushes the balloon forward. In a jet engine, the effect is almost the same. Air rushes through a tube. A spray of gasoline or kerosene is injected into the stream of air, and a series of continuous explosions takes place. The exploding gas creates a back pressure that sends the jet forward at great speed.

4. How does an airplane fly? If an airplane is standing on the ground, the air pressure on all its different parts is the same. This air pressure is increased or reduced when the airplane moves. There are four forces which act on an airplane as it flies through the air. The weight of the airplane, due to the earth's gravitation, tends to pull the airplane downward. Drag hinders the forward motion of the airplane. Drag is caused by the resistance the airframe offers as it moves through the air and by the eddies of air which form near edges of the lifting surfaces of the airplane. Weight and drag are overcome by thrust and lift. Thrust is provided by the engines which drive the airplane forward.

5. The upper surface of an airplane wing is cambered (curved upwards) at the leading edge and the under surface is almost flat to give the highest lift/drag ratio. This particular shape makes air flow faster and farther over the wing than under it. Pressure above

the wing is reduced and the wing is given lift. As the airplane moves forward, the air flowing over the wings produces lift to raise the airplane off the ground, and keep it in the air. The amount of lift increases with the speed of the airplane.

6. As jet airplanes were improved and began to go faster and faster, aeronautical engineers were forced to deal with a new problem. When a jet reaches the speed of sound-that is, about 700 miles an hour-an extreme pressure disturbance builds up just ahead of it. When a jet passes through this disturbance, we say that it is breaking the sound barrier, Jets that are able to fly faster than sound are called supersonic jets.

7. Concern about the supersonic jets has also been expressed by environmentalists. They are worried about atmospheric pollution that might be crested by the burning of fuel; and they are also worried about the sonic boom, which could be harmful to people and property. In fact, both economic and environmental arguments were brought to light when the United States Congress defeated a bill to continue funding for the development of a supersonic transport. All this means that the future of the commercial supersonic transport is not at all clear. It may well be that speed alone will not be the main emphasis in future aviation design.

8. The trend towards faster and larger airliners continues. The first jet airliners capable of supersonic speeds will carry more than one hundred passengers at two thousand, two hundred kilometers per hour (March 2.2). This is the maximum speed attainable by airplane with airframes made of conventional light alloys. Above Mach 2.2 the heat generated is so great that steel must be used. Airliners with airframes made of steel are being designed. They

will fly at Mach 3 or more. The streamlined nose sections of supersonic airliners will be 'dipped' during landing and take-off to provide better visibility for the pilot. Another innovation will be the use of 'variable geometry', whereby the wings will have two positions. The forward position will give maximum lift close to the ground while the rear position will give the best configuration for supersonic flight.

New Words and Expressions

aeronautics [ˌɛərəˈnɔːtiks] n. 航空学
airframe [ɛəfreim] n. 机身
altitude [ˈæltitjuːd] n. 高度,海拔
aviation [ˌeiviˈeiʃən] n. 航空,航空学
balloon [bəˈluːn] n. 气球
barrier [ˈbæriə] n. 障碍,栅栏
boom [buːm] n. 繁荣,隆隆声; vi. 急速发展; vt. 使兴旺
camber [ˈkæmbə] n. 弧形,(机翼的)弯曲度
clumsy [ˈklʌmzi] adj. 笨拙的,粗陋的
configuration [kənˌfigjuˈreiʃən] n. 外形,结构,形貌
craft [krɑːft] n. 技艺,手艺
crest [krest] n. 尖顶,顶峰,冠; v. 到达绝顶,加以顶饰
cruise [kruːz] vi. 巡游,巡航,漫游; n. 巡游,漫游,巡航
dip [dip] vt. 浸入,沉浸; vi. 倾斜,下倾,下降
drag [dræg] n. 拖,拖累; v. 拖动
eddy [ˈedi] n. 逆流,漩涡
explosion [iksˈpləuʒən] n. 爆炸(声),爆发
gasoline [ˈgæsəliːn] n. 汽油
grasp [grɑːsp] vt. 抓住,抓紧,掌握,领会; n. 抓住,理解,领会
hinder [ˈhində] adj. 后面的; v. 阻碍,打扰

inject [in'dʒekt] vt. 注射,注入,使入轨
jet [dʒet] n. 喷射,喷射流,喷嘴; v. 喷射,射出
kerosene ['kerəsi:n] n. 煤油
piston ['pistən] n. 活塞
pollution [pə'lu:ʃən,-'lju:-] n. 污染,玷污
propeller [prə'pelə] n. 螺旋桨,推进器
proportion [prə'pɔ:ʃən] n. 比例,比率,部分
rail [reil] n. 铁轨,栏杆
rear [riə] n. 后方,背后; adj. 后面的,背面的
rush [rʌʃ] n. 匆促,冲进,急流; vi. 冲,奔,涌现 vt. 使冲,匆忙地做
spray [sprei] n. 喷雾,飞沫; vt. 喷射,喷溅
streamline ['stri:mlain] n. 流线,流线型
supersonic ['sju:pəsɔnik] adj. 超声波的
variable ['vɛəriəbl] n. 变量,可变量
wing [wiŋ] n. 翅膀,机翼

Lesson 48

Communications Satellites

1. In a world that is becoming more and more interdependent, there is an ever-increasing need to link communications systems on various continents and to provide live international television coverage. This need is now being met by the communications satellites.

2. Communications satellites make use of technology that has been available for some time: the microwave radio relay. Microwaves, which have a higher frequency than ordinary radio waves, are used routinely in sending thousands of telephone calls and television programs across long distances. They give high-quality performance, and they can carry many messages at the same time.

3. But there has always been one problem in using radio relay in overseas communications. Although high-frequency waves can travel almost unlimited distances, they travel only in straight lines. Since the curvature of the earth limits a microwave's line-of-sight path to about 30 miles, good reception requires a series of relay towers spaced every 30 miles or so. Obviously it isn't possible to build these towers across the ocean. But by sending signals high up into the sky and then bouncing them back again to a far-off spot, we can send microwave messages long distances.

4. As long ago as 1945, Arthur C. Clarke, an English science-fiction writer, proposed that manned 'stationary' satellites be used to relay and broadcast electromagnetic communication signals. In 1945, of course, the idea of getting a satellite out into space seemed fantastic. But within ten years, satellites were close to reality. With the first launching of a satellite into orbit by the Soviet Union (*Sputnik I*) in 1957, the real development work on satellite communications began. Shortly thereafter, two successful satellites were launched in the United States, named as, *Echo I* and *Telstar I*.

5. The launching of the *Telstar I* satellite in 1962 marked a major step towards opening the era of commercial satellite communications. *Echo I*, a ten-story aluminum-coated balloon, was a 'passive' target; it merely reflected weak signals back to the earth. But *Telstar I* was the first "active" satellite to pick up a broadband signal, amplify it, and transmit it back to the earth on a different frequency. The satellite's transmission of transatlantic television thrilled millions.

6. A few months after *Telstar I* went into orbit, *Relay*, a medium-altitude satellite launched by the National Aeronautics and Space Administration (NASA), provided the first satellite communication between North and South America. *Relay* was followed by the *Telstar II* satellite, and by NASA's Syncom series and its successors - all of the high-altitude (23,000 miles) satellites whose orbits are synchronous with the rotation of the earth so that their positions, if they could be seen from the earth, would appear to be fixed in one spot.

7. Shortly before *Telstar I* was launched, the United States Congress established the Communications Satellite Corporation-

Comsat- to develop a commercial satellite system as part of an improved global communications network. Comsat, which is owned partly by public investors and partly by communications carriers, represents the United States in the International Telecommunications Satellite Consortium-Intelsat-and acts as manager for that body. Since its inception in 1962, the corporation, in collaboration with Intelsat, has inaugurated commercial satellite transmission of telephone, television, and other telecommunications traffic between North America and Europe and North America and the Fare East.

8. The commercial satellite *Intelsat IV* was launched in June of 1972. This one-and-one-half-ton spacecraft multiplied by five times the space-borne relaying capacity linking Africa, Europe, Asia, and Australia. With the launching of *Intelsat IV*, full global coverage by communications satellites had at last been achieved.

New Words and Expressions

aeronautics [ˌɛərə'nɔːtiks] *n*. 航空学
altitude ['æltitjuːd] *n*. 高度,海拔
borne [bɔːn] 'bear'的过去分词
bounce [bauns] *v*. (使)反跳,弹起,弹跳; *n*. 跳起,弹回
broadband ['brɔːdbænd] *n*. 宽频带,宽波段
communication [kəˌmjuːni'keiʃn] *n*. 通讯,交流
consortium [kən'sɔːtjəm] *n*. 协会,合伙,(国际性)财团
coverage ['kʌvəridʒ] *n*. 覆盖,覆盖的范围
curvature ['kəːvətʃə] *n*. 弯曲,曲率
electromagnetic [ilektrəu'mægnitik] *adj*. 电磁的
fiction ['fikʃən] *n*. 小说,虚构故事
frequency ['friːkwənsi] *n*. 频率

global ['gləubəl] *adj.* 球形的,全球的,通用的
inaugurate [i'nɔ:gjureit] *vt.* 开始,创始,开辟,举行…就职典礼
inception [in'sepʃən] *n.* 起初,创立,创办
interdependent [ˌintə(:)di'pendənt] *adj.* 相互依赖的
microwave ['maikrəuweiv] *n.* 微波
multiply ['mʌltipli] *v.* 乘;繁殖
network ['netwə:k] *n.* 网络,广播网
overseas ['əuvə:'si:z] *adj.* 海外的;*adv.* 在海外
passive ['pæsiv] *adj.* 被动的,消极的
radio ['reidiəu] *n.* 无线电,收音机
reception [ri'sepʃən] *n.* 接待,接受,招待会
relay ['ri:lei] *n.* 中继,接力,转播;*vt.* 使接替,给…接班
routine [ru:'ti:n] *n.* 常规,惯例
satellite ['sætəlait] *n.* 人造卫星
signal ['signl] *n.* 信号;*v.* 发信号;*adj.* 信号的
spacecraft ['speiskrɑ:ft] *n.* 航天飞船
spot [spɔt] *n.* 点,斑点,地点
stationary ['steiʃ(ə)nəri] *adj.* 不动的,稳态的,定常的
successor [sək'sesə] *n.* 后继者,继承人
synchronous ['siŋkrənəs] *n.* 同时的,同步的

Lesson 49

Travel into Outer Space

1. The rocket engine, with its steady roar like that of a waterfall or a thunderstorm, is an impressive symbol of the new space age. Rocket engines have proved powerful enough to shoot astronauts beyond the earth's gravitational pull and land them on the moon. We have now become travelers in space.

2. The rocket, which was invented in China over 800 years ago, is a relatively simple device. Fuel that is burned in the rocket engine changes into gas. The hot and rapidly expanding gas must escape, but it can do so only through an opening that faces backward. As the gas is ejected with great force, it pushes the rocket in the opposite direction. Like the kick of a gun when it is fired, it follows the laws of nature described by Sir Isaac Newton when he discovered that 'for every action, there is an equal and opposite reaction'.

3. There are many problems connected with space travel. The first and greatest of them is gravity. If you let your pencil drop to the floor, you can see gravity in action. Everything is held down to the earth by magnetic force. The weight of something is another way of describing the amount of force exerted on it by gravity. A rocket must go at least 2 500 miles an hour to take anyone beyond the gravity of the earth into space.

4. Another problem is the strain that a person is subjected to when a rocket leaves the ground. Anything that is not moving tends to resist movement. As the rocket leaves the ground, it pushes upward violently, and the person is pushed back against the chair. During this thrust, gravity exerts a force on the body equal to nine times its normal force.

5. Once out of the earth's gravity, an astronaut is affected by still another problem-weightlessness. Here, if a pencil drops, it does not fall. If a glass of water is turned upside down, the water will not fall out. All of us who are used to gravity expect things to have weight and to fall when dropped. Our bodies, which are accustomed to gravity, tend to become upset in weightless conditions. Recent long flights have shown that the body needs special exercise in a space ship.

6. Astronauts could also be affected by boredom and loneliness. Some of them might have to sit in their spaceships for months with little to do and no one to talk to. Space trips to distant planets or the nearest stars might take many years. It is possible that some trips might even take a lifetime. So future astronauts must be trained to endure long periods of inactivity and solitude.

7. Cosmic rays and tiny dust particles also raise a problem. Outer space, which has no air, is filled with both of these. The dust particles can damage the front end of the rapidly moving spaceship. The cosmic rays, though they are invisible to the naked eye, can go through the ship and the astronauts themselves. No one is sure what damage the cosmic rays can do to a human being, but scientists feel that brief exposure is probably not very harmful.

8. The intense heat caused by friction is also a problem in space travel. If you rub your hand hard on your forehead, you will feel this kind of heat. Once a spaceship is in outer space, there is no friction because there is no air to press against. But when the spaceship returns to the earth, it must go through air again. At first the air is very thin. But the closer the ship comes to the earth, the denser the air it meets. A spaceship entering the earth's atmosphere at full speed would get so hot that it would burn up completely and disappear.

9. Today, scientists are working harder than ever to solve the problems of space travel. In 1971, the Soviet Union sent into orbit the first experimental manned space station, Salyut 1. On May 14, 1973, the United States sent its first space station, Skylab 1, into orbit 270 miles above the earth. This laboratory in the sky, larger than a three-bedroom house, provided living quarters for three successive teams of three men each. These teams stayed in space for weeks at a time to perform various scientific experiments. One project was to survey some of the earth's surface in order to discover unknown natural resources, such as deposits of coal and oil. Another project was to map fault lines so that earthquakes can be predicted more accurately. Still another involved the observation of the atmospheric disturbances of the sun by telescope. These disturbances have an effect on the earth's weather. But the main purpose of Slylab was to find out how people could live and work in space for long periods of time.

New Words and Expressions

astronaut ['æstrənɔːt] n. 宇航员
atmosphere ['ætməsfiə] n. 大气,气氛

boredom ['bɔːdəm] n. 厌烦,厌倦
cosmic ['kɔzmik] adj. 宇宙的,宇宙航行的
dense [dens] adj. 密集的,浓厚的
disturbance [dis'təːbəns] n. 扰乱,不安
earthquake ['əːθkweik] n. 地震
eject [i'dʒekt] vt. 喷射,驱逐
endure [in'djuə] v. 忍受,忍耐,支持,持续
exposure [iks'pəuʒə] n. 暴露,揭露
friction ['frikʃən] n. 摩擦
invisible [in'vizəbl] adj. 看不见的
loneliness ['ləunlinis] n. 寂寞,孤独
magnetic [mæg'netik] adj. 磁的,有磁性的
orbit ['ɔːbit] n. 轨道;v. 绕…轨道而行
planet ['plænit] n. 行星,命运星辰
roar [rɔː] n. 吼叫,轰鸣,怒号; vi. 咆哮,吼叫;v. 滚动,咆哮
solitude ['sɔlitjuːd] n. 孤独,孤寂
telescope ['teliskəup] n. 望远镜
thrust [θrʌst] n. 插入,刺,推力,猛推;v. 猛推,插入,推进
tiny ['taini] adj. 微小的
violent ['vaiələnt] adj. 猛烈的,激烈的,暴力引起的,强暴的
violently adv. 猛烈地,激烈地
waterfall ['wɔːtəfɔːl] n. 瀑布

Lesson 50

Courses of Mechanics in UMIST

1. This prospectus is likely to be a first introduction to UMIST-the University of Manchester Institute of Science & Technology-an academic center known the world over, a place to broaden the mind, a community within a vigorous and cosmopolitan city, and a place to make friends and enjoy yourself. This brief introduction will give you an overall picture of a thriving center for learning, whose students are in demand in the job market and whose research projects play a vital role in world affairs.

2. **The University**

The University of Manchester Institute of Science and Technology was founded in 1824 in the days of the first Industrial Revolution and became incorporated as the Faculty of Technology in the University of Manchester shortly after the University received its charter in 1903. It has an academic staff of over 500 with a total student population of over 4,200 and occupies a site of 27 acres in the city center. Today it is one of the most famous and largest university-level institutions in the world.

3. UMIST courses are continually responding to the challenges of scientific developments. If you come here you will be at the forefront of exciting science and technology. In addition, the libraries, accommodation, health service and sport facilities

provided for UMIST students are good on campus and in the City too. Read this prospectus carefully and if you are interested either apply through the UCCA (the Universities Central Council on Admissions) scheme immediately or consult the Admissions Tutor in the Department of your choice.

4. **The Department**

The Department of Mechanical Engineering is one of the largest in UMIST with about 300 undergraduates, 125 postgraduates and 40 academic staff including 4 professors. There are also 100 supporting technical, administrative and research staff. The Department has always maintained close links with Industry, the Institution of Mechanical Engineers and with many Government and Educational Bodies. Research has always been an essential feature of the activities and all members of staff are currently engaged in both pure and applied research, much of this in collaboration with outside bodies. The Department obtains considerable financial support from industry and research organizations to pursue research. Recently the annual income from this source was about £2 million.

5. Although academic staff are mainly concerned with teaching and research they can also become involved as chairmen and members of committees related to an extremely wide range of activities. Through their membership staff can influence many related areas and advice can be effectively used. From the departmental point of view however, the importance is that the more active its staff are in these areas the more experience the department can draw upon in its deliberations for education and research policies. Many members of staff also act as consultants for industry and research organizations and are therefore able to

bring current engineering problems and developments into the context of the undergraduate course.

6. **Undergraduate Courses**

Undergraduate courses in the Department normally extend over three academic years, leading to the award of a BSc Honors Degree in Mechanical Engineering. The undergraduate courses are designed to educate students not only in a demanding academic discipline but also prepare them adequately for responsibility in their professional career after graduation. Undergraduates entering the Mechanical Engineering course follow, for the first two years, a basic common course in mechanical engineering and associated disciplines. In the third year there is a considerable freedom of choice of topics at two levels which enables more emphasis to be placed on chosen options.

7. **Course Content**

First year

Mathematics I, Engineering Mechanics I, Strength of Materials, Applied Thermodynamics I, Mechanics of Fluids I, Mechanical Engineering Laboratories, Engineering Drawing, Electrical Engineering and Laboratory, Materials Science I, Manufacturing Technology I, Tutorial Periods, Short courses in Computation, Optional Courses.

8. *Second Year*

Mathematics II, Engineering Mechanics II, Mechanics of Fluids II, Strength of Materials and Structures, Applied Thermodynamics II, Mechanical Engineering Laboratories, Engineering Design, Electrical Engineering and Laboratory, Materials Science II, Manufacturing Technology II, Tutorial Periods, Optional Courses.

9. *Third Year*

Elective Subjects (four or five subjects, depending upon level), selected from the following list:

'A' level

Elasticity-plasticity, Mechanics of Machines, Applied Thermodynamics, Engineering Fluid Mechanics, Theory of Metal Processes Friction and Lubrication, Machine Tool Engineering, Heat and Mass Transfer, Mechanics of Polymers and Composites, Automatic Control, Mathematics, Electrical Engineering, Quantitative Techniques and Operational Research.

10. 'B' level

Mechanics of Materials, Mechanics of Machines, Applied Thermodynamics, Engineering Fluid Mechanics, Quality Assurance, Environmental Pollution and Control, Heat and Mass Transfer, Mechanics of Polymers and Composites, Automatic control, Statistics, Electrical Engineering, Engineering in Medicine, Numerical Analysis, Applied Finite Element Analysis.

11. **Postgraduate Studies**

Modern engineering development requires staff trained beyond the level of a first degree and with experience in research and in the application of modern methods and techniques. The current high level of activity within the department in collaborative research has been maintained for many years, and over the past decade the number of registered postgraduate students has been in excess of 100. Thus the department is well endowed with both staff and equipment to provide the training, beyond the level of a first degree in research, as required by staff in the modern engineering industry.

12. **The degree of MSc and PhD by research**

The MSc course by research has a minimum duration of one calendar year and the PhD course a minimum duration of two years. Each student takes up an individual research investigation on which a Thesis has to be submitted. Subjects of research which are currently being pursued in the Department fall within the following fields: Applied Mechanics, Thermodynamics and Fluid Mechanics, Polymer Engineering and so on. More comprehensive details of research topics, publications, graduates and thesis titles are given in the Department's Annual Report of which copies are available on request.

13. **Degree of MSc by Examination and Dissertation**

Each course commences in October and has a minimum duration of one calendar year. The first two terms are spent on formal lectures and associated coursework. Written examinations are then held at about Easter and successful students proceed to the second part of the course, during which individual research topics are pursued and on which a dissertation has to be submitted.

14. **Diploma in Technical Science**

Each Diploma course is of one academic year's duration and comprises formal lecture courses, laboratory practice and a project on which a report has to be submitted. The courses are intended for candidates who are able to allow only nine months for their postgraduate training. The entry requirements are identical to those for MSc courses.

New Words and Expressions

academic [ˌækə'demik] *adj.* 学院的,学术的,理论的
accommodation [əˌkɔmə'deiʃən] *n.* 住处,膳宿

acre ['eikə] n. 英亩,地产
admission [əd'miʃən] n. 允许进入,许可入场(入学、入会),接纳,容纳
campus ['kæmpəs] n. <美>校园,大学教育
career [kə'riə] n. (原意:道路,轨道)事业,生涯
charter ['tʃɑːtə] n. 宪章; vt. 租,包(船、车等)
collaboration [kəˌlæbə'reiʃən] n. 协作,通敌
collaborative [kə'læbəreitiv] adj. 合作的,协作的
consult [kən'sʌlt] v. 商量,商议,请教,参考
consultant [kən'sʌltənt] n. 顾问,商议者,咨询者
context ['kɔntekst] n. 上下文,文章的前后关系
cosmopolitan [ˌkɔzmə'pɔlitən] adj. 世界性的,国际的,全球(各地)的
council ['kaunsil] n. 政务会,理事会,委员会,参议会,顾问班子
course [kɔːs] n. 课程,过程,进程,跑道
deliberation [diˌlibə'reiʃən] n. 熟思,从容,商议,考虑
diploma [di'pləumə] n. 文凭,毕业证书,证明权力、特权、荣誉等的证书、奖状
discipline ['disiplin] n. 纪律,学科; v. 训练
dissertation [ˌdisə(ː)'teiʃən] n. (学位)论文,专题,论述
environmental [inˌvaiərən'mentl] adj. 周围的,环境的; n. 环境论
friction ['frikʃən] n. 摩擦,摩擦力
identical [ai'dentikəl] adj. 同一的,同样的
investigation [inˌvesti'geiʃən] n. 调查,研究
lubrication [ˌluːbri'keiʃən] n. 润滑油
manufacture [ˌmænju'fæktʃə] vt. 制造,加工; n. 制造,制造业,产品
operational [ˌɔpə'reiʃənl] adj. 操作的,运作的

operational research 运筹学
pollution [pə'lu:ʃən,-'lju:-] n. 污染；玷污
polymer ['pɔlimə] n. 聚合体
postgraduate ['pəust'grædjuit,'pəust'grædʒuit] n. 研究生；adj. 毕业后的
prospectus [prəs'pektəs] n. 内容说明书，章程，简介
pursue [pə'sju:] vt. 追赶，追踪，继续，从事
quantitative ['kwɔntitətiv] adj. 数量的，定量的
staff [stɑ:f] n. 全体职员；棒，杆，支柱
statistics [stə'tistiks] n. 统计学，统计表
submit [səb'mit] vt. 提交，递交
thermodynamics ['θə:məudai'næmiks] n. [物] 热力学
thesis ['θi:sis] n. 论题，论文
thrive [θraiv] v. 兴旺，繁荣，茁壮成长，旺盛
undergraduate [ˌʌndə'grædjuit] n. (尚未取得学位的)大学生；adj. 大学生的
vigorous ['vigərəs] adj. 精力旺盛的，有力的，健壮的

参 考 文 献

[1] STEPHEN P, TIMOSHENKO, JAMES M. Mechanics of Materials[M]. New York; Cincinnati; London; Chicago: Van Nostrand Reinhold Company, 1972

[2] NAM P S, ARTHUR P L T. Elements of the Mechanical Behavior of Solids[M]. Washington, D. C.: Scripta Book Company, 1975

[3] ROBERT M J. Mechanics of Composite Materials[M]. Scripta Book Company, 1975

[4] EWER J R, LATORRE G. A Course in Basic Scientific English[M]. London: Longman Group Limited, 1976

[5] THORNLEY G C. Elementary Scientific English Practice [M]. London: Longman Group Limited, 1977

[6] HERBERT A J. The Structure of Technical English[M]. London: Longmans. Freen and Co Ltd, 1965

[7] OWEN D R J, FAWKES A J. Engineering Fracture Mechanics[M]. Swansea: Pineridge Press Ltd, 1983